CLOSING METHODOLOGICAL DIVIDES

Philosophy and Education

VOLUME 11

SCOPE OF THE SERIES

There are many issues in education that are highly philosophical in character. Among these issues are the nature of human cognition; the types of warrant for human beliefs; the moral and epistemological foundations of educational research; the role of education in developing effective citizens; and the nature of a just society in relation to the educational practices and policies required to foster it. Indeed, it is difficult to imagine any issue in education that lacks a philosophical dimension.

The sine qua non of the volumes in the series is the identification of the expressly philosophical dimensions of problems in education coupled with an expressly philosophical approach to them. Within this boundary, the topics—as well as the audiences for which they are intended—vary over a broad range, from volumes of primary interest to philosophers to others of interest to a more general audience of scholars and students of education.

The titles published in this series are listed at the end of this volume.

Closing Methodological Divides
Toward Democratic Educational Research

by

KENNETH R. HOWE
University of Colorado,
Boulder, CO, U.S.A.

KLUWER ACADEMIC PUBLISHERS
DORDRECHT / BOSTON / LONDON

A C.I.P. Catalogue record for this book is available from the Library of Congress.

ISBN 1-4020-1164-4 (HB)
ISBN 1-4020-1226-8 (PB)

Published by Kluwer Academic Publishers,
P.O. Box 17, 3300 AA Dordrecht, The Netherlands.

Sold and distributed in North, Central and South America
by Kluwer Academic Publishers,
101 Philip Drive, Norwell, MA 02061, U.S.A.

In all other countries, sold and distributed
by Kluwer Academic Publishers,
P.O. Box 322, 3300 AH Dordrecht, The Netherlands.

Printed on acid-free paper

Printed in the Netherlands.

*This book is dedicated to the
ideal of educational research
as an instrument of
progressive social change.*

Contents

Preface

The issues I treat in this book—qualitative versus quantitative methods, facts versus values, science versus politics, subjectivity versus objectivity, postmodernism versus pragmatism, to name a few—are at the core of a lively, sometimes divisive, conversation that has been unfolding in the theory and practice of educational research for some time. These issues fall squarely within the province of philosophy, and thus philosophical investigation has an especially useful contribution to make. But these issues are by no means the exclusive province of philosophy; they are ones in which a diverse group of educational theorists have had a keen interest and about which they have had important things to say. The conversation I hope to join—and to move forward—is this broad and inclusive one. Philosophy of education is at its best when it dives headlong into the fray.

The book borrows liberally from my previously published work, but is far from a simple compilation. The ideas developed in Chapter 7, "On the Threat of Epistemological Bias," are new. The ideas developed in Chapter 9, "Toward Democratic Educational Research," are a significant extension of the application of similar ideas to evaluation research. The ideas developed in Chapter 4, "The Persistence of the Fact/Value Dogma," are in a form and at a level of detail not published before. Finally, Chapter 1, "Introduction and Overview," weaves together my thinking on a large array of issues on educational research methodology that had only been loosely connected before. The remaining chapters range from minor to significant revisions of the work from which they derive, and I often combined things in new ways. As the description of Chapter 1 suggests, I made a concerted effort to get the chapters to hang together and to build on one another so as to form an integral whole.

Acknowledgments

Several people deserve thanks for their feedback on specific chapters: Margaret Eisenhart, Pamela Courtenay Hall, and Michele Moses (Chapter 7); Ernie House, Bill McGinley and Nick Peressini (Chapter 6); and Ernie House (Chapter 9). Damian Betebenner and Sam Foster provided feedback on the entire manuscript. The two anonymous reviewers arranged by Kluwer provided a wealth of useful feedback, particularly regarding Chapters 1, 4, and 9. I thank them for their efforts. I also thank my co-authors on articles that I have used as the basis for several chapters: Jason Berv (Chapter 6), Margaret Eisenhart (Chapter 3), and Michele Moses (Chapter 8). I was careful to use only the arguments and words that were originally mine, but a few of their sentences may have slipped in. Of course, there is no way to eliminate the effects of their collaboration on my thinking, nor would I want to.

Below I acknowledge the publishers of my previous works in terms of the positions of these works in the chapters of the book. Chapter 2 is a revised and abridged version of Howe, K. (1985), Two dogmas of educational research, *Educational Researcher, 14*(8), 10–18. Chapter 3 is a revised version of Howe, K. (1988), Against the quantitative–qualitative incompatibility thesis (or dogmas die hard), *Educational Researcher, 17*(8), 10–16. Chapter 3 also incorporates a revised and abridged version of a section of Howe, K. and Eisenhart, M. (1990), Standards in qualitative (and quantitative) research: a prolegomenon, *Educational Researcher, 9*(4), 2–9. Chapter 4 is an earlier and more extensive version of what became Chapter 3, "The Received View," in House, E. & Howe, K. (1999), *Values in evaluation and social research*, Thousand Oaks, CA: Sage. Chapter 4 also incorporates revised portions of Howe, K., "The Technical Approach to Social Research, and What's Wrong With It," RACE 2000 Conference, Tempe, AZ (January 2000). Chapter 5 is a minor revision of Howe, K. (1998), The interpretive turn and the new debate in education, *Educational Researcher, 27*(8), 13–21. Chapter 6 is a revised and abridged version of Howe, K. & Berv, J. (2000), Constructing constructivism, epistemological and pedagogical, in D.C. Phillips (Ed.), *Constructivism in education: Opinions and second opinions on controversial issues* (Ninety-ninth Yearbook of the National Society for the Study of Education) (pp. 19–40), Chicago: the National Society for the Study of Education. Chapter 8 is a revised and abridged version of Howe, K. & Moses, M. (1999), Ethics in educational research, in A. Iran-Nejad & P. D. Pearson Eds., the *Review of Research in Education*, vol. 24, pp. 21–60, Washington, D.C.: American Educational Research Association.

I end these acknowledgments with heartfelt thanks to my wife, Tonda, for her unwavering support and for always being so full of life.

Chapter 1

INTRODUCTION AND OVERVIEW

The interpretivist methodological framework made its appearance in educational research in the late 1970's. Thus began a fundamental and far-reaching challenge to the dominance of the positivist methodological framework. Much scholarly effort in this vein has been devoted to excavating methodological divides. This book is devoted to closing them.

Following this introductory chapter, Chapters 2-7 are divided into two major parts: *Positivism and the Old Divides* (Chapters 2–4) and *Interpretivism and the New Divides* (Chapters 5–7). The shift from Part I to Part II marks the changed boundaries of the general methodological conversation associated with the coming of age of interpretive—or "qualitative"—educational research. As interpretivist educational research gained widespread acceptance and credibility, it, rather than positivism, began to set the terms of debate. The old divides *between* interpretivism and positivism began to disappear, only to be replaced by new divides *within* interpretivism.

Chapters 8 and 9 comprise Part III, *Ethical and Political Frameworks.* Chapter 8 revisits the shift from Part I to Part II in terms of the protection of human subjects, a central concern in the ethics of social research. The ninth and concluding chapter proffers a conception of democratic educational research, building on what has come before.

The descriptions of the chapters to follow provide thumbnail sketches of the major arguments of each chapter and suggest how they fit together so as to point in the general direction of a democratic conception of educational research. The details of the arguments in support of the many controversial claims I make will have to wait for the chapters themselves.

Part I: Positivism and the Old Divides

The influence of positivism on educational research methodology has been significant, and it spawned two stubborn dogmas: the quantitative/qualitative dogma and the fact/value dogma.

The quantitative/qualitative dogma construes the distinction between quantitative and qualitative research methods as presupposing a distinction between two radically different—and incompatible—epistemological stances: quantitative methods presuppose a positivist epistemology; qualitative methods presuppose an interpretivist one. The fact/value dogma construes the distinction between facts and values as marking a distinction between two radically different domains of knowledge, or, more accurately, between what lies within the domain of knowledge and what does not. The fact/value dogma is shorthand for a more general divide: the fact side of the divide includes rationality, science, means, cognition, objectivity and truth; the value side includes irrationality, politics, ends, interests, subjectivity and power.

These ways of construing the quantitative/qualitative and fact/value distinctions deserve the name the "two dogmas" because they are each based on the unexamined assumption that positivism is still a serious competitor among epistemological views. Chapter 2 criticizes this assumption.

Positivism embraces a rigid distinction between the theoretical or conceptual contents of knowledge claims, on the one hand, and their observational contents, on the other. It then presupposes this distinction in setting a very strict standard for empirical knowledge, namely, that it be grounded in *neutral* or *brute* observational data. But critics successfully demolished this standard of knowledge—*verificationism*— long ago, by establishing that the observational contents of knowledge cannot be separated from the conceptual contents in the way verificationism requires. Instead, observational and conceptual contents interpenetrate one another.

The collapse of positivism undermines the quantitative/qualitative dogma, for the forced choice the dogma sets up assumes that positivism is one of the epistemological alternatives to be adopted. But, or so the argument goes, positivism is not an alternative, at least not a defensible one. The collapse of positivism undermines the fact/value dogma as well, for this dogma is but a corollary of positivism's verificationist epistemology. That is, positivism excludes values from the domain of knowledge because values fail to measure up to the standard for knowledge positivism sets. Because this standard is untenable, so is the idea that values should be (or can be) culled from the practice of knowledge production. Just as conceptual contents penetrate empirical knowledge claims, so do values. This interpenetration of empirical knowledge and values—the *value-ladeness* of empirical knowledge—is especially salient in social and educational research, whose vocabulary is rooted in the description of social practices and whose aim is to evaluate and improve such practices.

The initial critique of the two dogmas proffered in Chapter 2 is extended and refined in the two chapters that follow.

Chapter 3 examines the ways in which the descriptors "quantitative" and "qualitative" are applied at three levels of research practice: data, design and analysis, and interpretation of results. Because there is no fundamental incompatibility between quantitative and qualitative methods at any of these levels, there is no discernible reason to avoid combining them.

Chapter 3 next examines the alleged incompatibility between the epistemological paradigms that are supposed to underlie quantitative and qualitative methods. This strand of argument digs more deeply into the (dogmatic) thesis, introduced in Chapter 2, of a forced choice between positivism and interpretivism.

Not only is positivism moribund, so are certain early versions of interpretivism that emphasize understanding the insider's interpretations to the exclusion of everything else. These versions of interpretivism have given way to more complicated interpretivist (or interpretivist-inspired) approaches that incorporate the idea of an interplay or "dialectical tacking" (Geertz, 1979) between the expert social scientific (or *positivist*) perspective and the insider's (or *interpretivist*) perspective. Although classic forms of positivism and interpretivism are, indeed, incompatible, epistemological work has not stood still. Elements of these classic forms may be combined in a pragmatic "compatibilist" view.

Chapter 4 provides a sustained critique of the fact/value dogma, beginning with the observation that it is as entrenched as ever in social and educational research, so much so that it qualifies as the "received view." The chapter builds its arguments on two examples: one from evaluation research, where the received view is explicitly elaborated and defended, and one from educational measurement, where it is presupposed.

Donald Campbell (1982) provides one articulation of the received view in evaluation research. For him, value claims, unlike factual claims, are "radically undecidable" (House & Howe, 1999) —they cannot be "justified." That values have no epistemological standing is one reason to jettison them from social research, according to Campbell. A related reason is that their inclusion contributes to bias. Campbell's view is firmly—and openly— rooted in the positivistic construal of the fact/value distinction. It is very dubious for that reason. (Campbell's views on this point are treated in greatest detail in Chapter 2.)

But things moved on, as theorists attempted to distance themselves from an open embrace of the positivist conception of the fact/value distinction. In this vein, a contemporary version of the received view in evaluation research is exemplified by Shadish, Cook and Leviton (1995). They emphasize "practical" rather than epistemological reasons for culling value commitments out of evaluation research. For example, they observe that little agreement exists on what is right or just, and that incorporating positions on such issues into the conduct, conclusions, and recommendations of research compromises its ability to influence policy.

The critique of Shadish et al. zeros in on their descriptive-prescriptive dichotomy. First, building on the arguments of Chapter 2, the descriptive versus prescriptive elements of social research cannot be disentangled. Here, Shadish et al. exhibit some positivist backsliding, as it were. For, contra positivism, values (prescriptive elements) enter into what questions are deemed worth investigating and whose views should be heard. They are also implicit in the very vocabulary that social research employs, as in "achievement" or "oppression," for instance.

Second, Shadish et al. argue as if they were providing an *alternative to employing a prescriptive theory* when they are actually *employing a prescriptive theory of their own*. That is, they clearly *prescribe* how evaluators should practice their craft. In particular, they admonish them to confine themselves to "descriptive valuing"—describing the values of stakeholders—and to avoid "prescriptive valuing"—prescribing what is right or just. In this way, Shadish et al. implicitly embrace a certain conception of political decision-making, "emotive democracy" (House & Howe, 1999). Consistent with the view that values are radically undecidable, this conception construes all value claims as immune from rational examination and thus on a par. This precludes the received view from embracing a methodology that would mitigate the gross inequalities of resources and the associated imbalances of power that characterize the current political scene. Indeed, it explicitly rejects such a methodology. In outcome if not design, Shadish et al's approach serves the political status quo.

The "consequentialist" conception of validity in educational measurement closely parallels the received view in evaluation research. The basic idea is that various uses of testing have consequences that can be good or bad, and that these must be included in determining whether a test is valid. But advocates of the consequentialist conception stop short of making any judgments about what consequences are actually good or bad and about what political principles should be used to make such determinations. Instead, they (Shepard, 1993, for example) distinguish "purely value choices" from what "scientific investigation" can tell us and then present us with hypotheticals on the model of Shadish et al's "value summaries"—Test X is valid, *if* you want to promote value Y.

The received view in evaluation and the consequentialist conception in educational measurement each has the self-perception that it rejects "value-freedom" and addresses values in social research. But values aren't really *addressed* at all; they are listed and then conditionally linked to factual (or "scientific") claims. This is a timid way to handle values in educational research. If it moves beyond the positivist fact/value dogma at all, it does so only slightly.

The end of Chapter 4 marks the end of Part I, *Positivism and the Old Divides*, but there is continuity between it and Part II, *Interpretivism and the New Divides*.

For one thing, the received view continues to be widely held across the broad spectrum of educational research. So, there is continuity in the sense that positivism, or at least one of its central tenets, persists.

There is also continuity in another sense, one central to the analysis of Chapters 5–7. In particular, there are two different conclusions that may be drawn from the kind of thoroughgoing rejection of positivism that includes also rejecting the fact/value dogma. For some, who I call "postmodernists," the implication is that *both* facts and values are radically undecidable; for others, who I call "transformationists," the implication is that *neither* facts nor values are radically undecidable. Much of Part II may be seen as a defense of the transformationist view against the postmodernist one (though not always in those terms).

Part II: Interpretivism and the New Divides

The epistemology of social science witnessed an "interpretive turn" in the last quarter of the 20th century (Rabinow & Sullivan, 1979). Although an important faction of the educational research community put up heavy resistance (this is what the old divide *between* quantitative and qualitative research was all about), interpretive methodology eventually secured its place. One of the outcomes of this success has been the opening of new divides *within* the interpretivist methodological paradigm. Chapter 5 identifies three areas of controversy—epistemology, the ontology of the self, and politics—and associates the different positions taken in these areas with two general stances alluded to above: "postmodernist" and "transformationist."

The controversy about epistemology centers on whether, after abandoning positivist epistemology, there is any way to make sense out of the concept of knowledge except as radically contingent, local, and a mere conduit for the expression of power. Postmodernists seem to deny this possibility. They are especially critical of grand "meta-narratives"—the inevitable progress of science, Marxism, liberalism—which they believe can have no grounding except in power relationships and can only serve to oppress and "terrorize" people. Transformationists criticize postmodernists for their alleged commitment to a strong and untenable form of relativism.

Transformationists, too, reject positivist epistemology, but they deny this implies also rejecting the idea that there can be criteria of knowledge that are distinguishable from power interests. Postmodernists themselves must presuppose such criteria, lest their claims merely express *their* power interests and thus provide no reason for anyone who doesn't already agree to be persuaded by what they say.

Regarding the ontology of the self, postmodernists and transformations agree in rejecting the idea of an essential human nature. Each believes that identities are contingent and are formed in norm-sanctioned social encounters. The primary difference lies in their respective attitudes toward "normalization." Postmodernists see any induction of persons into norms as sinister and oppressive, and to be resisted and thrown off by them. Transformationists hold the view that although inducting persons into norms can be "dangerous," as Foucault says, it is unavoidable. Furthermore, there are forms of normalization that are good and that the practice of education should promote. Educating students so that they are disposed to recognize and resist oppression is one type of "normalization" that postmodernists themselves would seem committed to.

This leads naturally into the issue of politics. Postmodernists, especially among educationists, see themselves as the enemies of oppression. But this requires a view of knowledge that enables them to identify and condemn oppression. They don't have such a view; the transformationists do. According to the latter, although the findings of social research may be distorted by imbalances of power, social research is redeemable to the extent these distorting influences can be identified and held in check.

Chapter 6 coins the term "constructivist turn" in order to call attention to fundamental parallels between constructivist and interpretivist epistemology. Both reject positivist epistemology; both construe knowledge as actively constructed by agents rather than as passively received by them; both raise fundamental issues concerning subjectivism and relativism; and both have engendered internecine divides. In the case of the constructivist turn, the divide is between "post-Kantian constructivists" and "radical constructivists."

As its name suggests, post-Kantian constructivism has in roots in the epistemology of the 18th century German philosopher Immanuel Kant, who held that experience is always shaped or *constructed* by the mind's categories. *Post-*Kantian constructivism came about as a consequence of the 20th century "linguistic turn," in which language assumed the role previously occupied by Kant's categories. As in Ludwig Wittgenstein's "language games," W.V.O. Quine's "conceptual schemes," and Thomas Kuhn's "paradigms," language became the vehicle through which experience (or meaning) is shaped or *constructed.*

Radical constructivism starts at different place from post-Kantian constructivism, epistemologically speaking. Rather than starting with shared meanings that shape individual experiences, as post-Kantian constructivism does, it starts with individuals' experiences and builds up a language of shared meanings from there. In this, and ironically it would seem, radical constructivism is a close cousin of positivism. Both assume that *fundamentally private* experiences exist—whose meaning and content is available only to the individuals who have these experiences—and that these comprise the material from which shared meanings must be constructed. Radical constructivism winds up mired in solipsism, the most extreme form of relativism. By being so radical as to take the idea of the construction of experience/meaning all the way down to the level of individuals, it results in stranding individuals in worlds of their own making. Radical constructivism fails to recognize and embrace a core tenet of constructivism, from Kant onwards: that knowledge construction must *start* with shared categories, language games, conceptual schemes, paradigms, or the like.

To be sure, post-Kantian constructivism also faces the threat of relativism. For the world is made up of many different groups of people who play many different language games and many different of language games. Chapter 6 devotes some attention to responding to this charge, in general, and to the form it assumes in social science, in particular. The work of pragmatists and near pragmatists, such as Kuhn, Quine, Rorty, and especially Putnam, are employed to suggest that the charge of relativism may be successfully fended off when it comes to post-Kantian constructivism. At least the charge of relativism is much less damaging to post-Kantian than to radical constructivism.

Chapter 6 ends by tying constructivist epistemology more closely to the other meanings of "constructivism" in education, including educational research. It provides a brief sketch of "thoroughgoing constructivism," a Deweyan view that integrates constructivist epistemology with constructivist approaches to learning, curriculum, and pedagogy, and with constructivist approaches to social research. At the same time that thoroughgoing constructivism integrates the various kinds of constructivism, it also sees a "looseness of fit" among them, such that the overarching epistemology, not teaching or research methods in isolation, determines whether an approach is truly a constructivist one.

Chapter 7 examines the idea of "epistemological bias:" what "epistemological bias" means, how pervasive it is, and what is to be done about it. The need to ask these questions has been stimulated by the postmodernist/transformationist divide, and the answers provided fall on either side.

The point of departure for the analysis is the provocative—indeed, startling—thesis advanced by James Scheurich and Michelle Young (1997) that virtually all epistemological frameworks underpinning educational research are biased (racially biased in particular). This represents the postmodernist side of the divide, and it does not hold up well under scrutiny.

I frame the analysis in terms of three questions: What is bias? What is epistemology? and What is biased epistemology? Here I make a few remarks about the second two of these questions.

Epistemology may be defined as the "study of the nature of knowledge and justification" (Moser, 1995). Implicit in this definition is a distinction between the normative and the descriptive elements of epistemology, between how knowledge *ought* to be conceived and how it is *in fact* conceived.

Epistemological investigation from Plato to the positivists has involved the interplay between these two elements. But the epistemological project in which they were engaged—of identifying the ultimate *foundations* of knowledge that must be the same for all times, all places, and all people—was largely rejected in the mid 20th century as impossible to pull off.

One outcome was a challenge to the normative/descriptive distinction itself, taken up by neo-Nietzschian (postmodernist) thinkers such as Michel Foucault. On this view, *anti*-epistemology, as it has been called, knowledge is grounded in time and place and the "regimes of truth" that predominate; knowledge is, in effect, but an expression of power and is thereby divested of its normative dimension. Scheurich and Young (1997) apply such an anti-epistemological view to educational research in particular. Their rejection of the normative/descriptive distinction is manifested in their general thesis that all epistemologies in educational research are biased because they are all outgrowths of "civilizational racism."

The outstanding problem with this thesis is its vacuity. If all epistemologies are biased simply because they have a history, then the idea of a "biased epistemology"—and presumably biased is a bad thing for an epistemology to be—loses its meaning. For there is no history-less perspective from which to make the claim that one epistemology is any more or less biased than another.

The aim of Chapter 7 is not to dismiss the idea of biased epistemology, but to find an illuminating account of it. In this vein, *anti*-epistemology is not the only response to abandoning the overly ambitious aspirations of epistemology. *Post*-epistemology is another response, and one that is widely embraced by thinkers who endeavor to preserve a place for the normative element of epistemology. This view, which is critical of the anti-epistemological (or postmodernist) view, holds that without the normative element, there is no perspective from which *epistemology-in-use*—the epistemological principles that are in fact employed in the conduct of social and educational research—may be critically evaluated.

Interpretivists, such as Charles Taylor, as well as feminist "standpoint" theorists, such as Sandra Harding, exemplify the post-epistemological view. Unlike Scheurich and Young, rather than making an omnibus genetic argument against virtually any epistemological perspective, these thinkers zero-in on positivistic epistemology of social research.

In particular, positivistic social research is biased against certain cultural and racial groups, as well as against women, because of its penchant to employ pre-interpreted categories which are the creations of researchers and which have no grounding in the social meanings of the people being studied. The problem is exacerbated by the fact that the community of social researchers has typically excluded the groups to whom the pre-interpreted categories are being applied in a biased fashion. Chapter 7 ends with the suggestion that the way to control bias in social and educational research is through the principle of inclusion. This principle has both methodological and moral dimensions. Good methodology requires that samples include an adequate representation of all groups for whom generalizations are intended. After the interpretive turn, good methodology also requires that the genuine voices of various groups should be a part of this, not just what the researcher deems as germane. And this requirement—for *thick* inclusion—shades well into to the ethical requirement that participants in social and educational research have a voice in how their lives are described and how they might be improved.

Part III: Ethical and Political Frameworks

Chapter 8 revisits the general shift from positivism to interpretivism in terms of research ethics. It is framed in terms of the "traditional problematic"—which emphasizes protecting autonomy—and the "contemporary problematic"— which emphasizes coming to grips with the complexities wrought by the emphasis on (thick) inclusion.

The traditional problematic is an outgrowth of experimentalist research. It construes the protection of human subjects narrowly, in terms of ensuring subjects are provided with the opportunity to give or withhold their informed consent to participate. Although it provides more exacting standards for members of "vulnerable populations" whose ability to consent is in doubt, for example, children and prisoners, it otherwise assumes that consent from mentally competent adults is relatively unproblematic and renders research in which they agree to participate unproblematic as well.

The contemporary problematic is an outgrowth of the advent of interpretivist research, as well as related developments in moral and political philosophy. Interpretive (or "qualitative") research is more "intimate" in its methods and "open-ended" in its design and conduct than experimentalist research (e.g., Howe & Dougherty, 1993). This complicates protecting research subjects through the mechanism of informed consent. In moral and political philosophy, care theory, communitarianism, postmodernism, and critical theory increasingly challenge the liberal theory that underpins the traditional problematic and its central principle of autonomy.

The interpretive turn has resulted in a significant break between the traditional and the contemporary problematics. But there is also a significant continuity. Contemporary liberal philosophers such as Will Kymlicka (1991) have done much to repair the damage done to liberalism by its critics, particularly by emphasizing the complex social and cultural factors that go into defining the "context of choice" that facilitates or blunts the exercise of autonomy. Furthermore, a certain "looseness of fit" characterizes the relationship between broad philosophical views—care theory, communitarianism, critical theory, and liberalism—and the principles and procedures that guide the protection of research subjects. Chapter 8 advances the thesis that despite otherwise fundamental changes in the methodology of educational research, protecting autonomy remains the fundamental principle of research ethics, and informed consent remains its procedural embodiment.

Chapter 9 is the capstone of the book. It builds on major themes with an eye toward bringing them together in support of democratic educational research. Its point of departure is the rejection of the fact/value dogma, especially the "emotive" conception of democracy that is heavily criticized in Chapter 4. Chapter 9 offers the alternative, "deliberative" conception, which is fleshed out in terms of three principles: *inclusion, dialogue,* and *deliberation* (House & Howe, 1999).

Inclusion ranges from *passive* to *active,* from, say, filling out a fixed-response survey instrument to engaging in an open-ended discussion. Inclusion is both a methodological principle (representative sampling) and a democratic principle (the right to have ones views included in forums that have a bearing on social life).

Active inclusion shades into dialogue, the second principle. Dialogue also has a range: from *elucidating* (getting the diversity of *emic* perspectives on the table) to *critical* (subjecting *emic* perspectives to critical examination, as appropriate). Dialogue, too, is both a methodological and a democratic requirement. It is a methodological requirement of interpretivist research that seeks to ascertain social reality from the point of view of the actors who construct and participate in it. It is a democratic requirement because, like the principle of inclusion, all views should be included in forums that have a bearing on social life. In comparison to (passive) inclusion, however, dialogue is presumably better able to yield *genuine* views.

Deliberation, the third principle, is a species of critical dialogue. It fits with a conception of democratic decision-making that differs not only from the emotive conception, but also from the conception that restricts dialogue to elucidation. The latter approach—"hyper-egalitarianism" (House & Howe, 1999) —aspires to foster equality in dialogue among research participants, but it perverts the idea of *genuine voice* by not paying attention to the conditions out of which it can emerge. It focuses exclusively on researchers as the source of bias and the abuse of power and limits their role to that of mere facilitators who must never challenge participants' views and who must eschew expert knowledge (e.g., Guba & Lincoln, 1989).

But when people enter into dialogue about educational policies, they can be mistaken or misinformed about the harms and benefits of various educational policies, including to themselves. Simply clarifying how they think things work, and ought to work, can be no more than one element of genuine deliberation. Deliberation includes clarifying the views and self-understandings of research participants but also subjecting these views and self-understandings to rational scrutiny. Deliberation is a critical activity in which participants and researchers collaboratively engage and from which the most rationally defensible conclusions emerge.

Once again, methodological and democratic principles dovetail. Deliberation is required, methodologically, to ensure that the most accurate portrayal of social arrangements emerges. Deliberation is required, democratically, to insure that power imbalances, including in knowledge and the resources to garner it, do not tilt—or "distort"—the dialogue so as to advantage the already advantaged. Educational researchers have a fiduciary responsibility in this regard (House & Howe, 1999).

The spectrum of topics investigated by educational research is broad and so are the political conditions under which it must be conducted. Thus, the conception of democratic educational research adumbrated in Chapter 9 must be seen as an ideal, and one more easily employed in educational policy research than in research on pedagogy (a point I spend some time developing). Still, all educational research bears *some* relationship to democracy, a fact that is all too often ignored.

I end the book with a few observations about how the general pragmatic themes of Chapters 2 through 8 complement the conception of democratic educational research sketched in Chapter 9.

Pragmatism abandons the quest for ultimate epistemological foundations and holds that knowledge is a human construction. But it also holds that truth, objectivity, democracy, justice, and the like, are indispensable and redeemable ideals, without which we fall into a hopeless kind of relativism. Pragmatism blurs the edges among empirical research methodologies. It evaluates them not by *a priori* epistemological standards, but by the epistemological standard of their fruitfulness in *use*. Most radically, perhaps, pragmatism also blurs the edges between methodology and moral-political principles. In particular, educational research methodology cannot be evaluated apart from its relationship to democratic aims.

I

POSITIVISM AND THE OLD DIVIDES

Chapter 2

TWO DOGMAS OF EDUCATIONAL RESEARCH

It has been nearly 50 years since W.V.O. Quine published "Two Dogmas of Empiricism," in which he demolished the two central tenets[1] of logical positivism.[2] The educational research community was slow to respond to the implications. Instead, it continued to labor under two invidious positivistic dogmas of its own: the quantitative/qualitative dogma and the fact/value dogma.

The distinctions between quantitative and qualitative methods and between facts and values do mark important differences, but these differences do not constitute deep, unbridgeable divides. In this chapter, I argue that the rigidity with which these distinctions have been conceived in late twentieth century thinking about educational research methodology is based on dogmas held over from logical positivism that have been long since repudiated.

The chapter is divided into three sections. In the first, I identify the quantitative/qualitative dogma with a forced choice between quantitative and qualitative methods. Such a forced choice is unnecessary for two reasons. First, the positivist notion that qualitative data is inherently subjective and therefore untrustworthy is untenable. The argument in this section supports Campbell's (1974, 1979) view that social research is based on "qualitative knowing" and that quantification extends, refines, and crosschecks qualitative knowledge. Second, two additional positivist tenets are untenable: (a) scientific inference is mechanical (i.e., involves no extra-theoretical, extra-observational, qualitative judgment) and (b) inference in social research is the same as inference in natural science. I advance the alternative view that qualitative judgments are required in making scientific inferences of any kind but are especially prominent in social research.

In the second section, I entertain two reasons for embracing the fact/value dogma: positivistic epistemology and the desire to avoid value bias. I contend that a rigid epistemological distinction between facts and values is no more defensible than the positivistic tenets upon which it is based, and that employing the fact/value distinction to avoid value bias instead exacerbates the danger of bias by submerging rather than eliminating value commitments.

In the third and concluding section, I discuss the broad practical implications of abandoning the two dogmas. Briefly, counterproductive debates about what research method is best per se are obviated; the dangerous notion that educational research is, ought to, or can be value-free is repudiated; and researchers are freed from choosing exclusively between a descriptive, quantitative approach and a value-laden, qualitative one.

Dogma 1: The Quantitative/Qualitative Distinction

The ascendance of positivism prompted a debate in philosophy of social science about whether social research should employ the epistemological paradigm portrayed and advocated by positivism, or whether it should employ an alternative "interpretive" paradigm of its own. This debate set the terms of the subsequent debate about quantitative versus qualitative research methods. The positivist paradigm was identified with quantitative methods and the interpretive paradigm was identified with qualitative methods, and two positions were advanced regarding the relationship between research methods and epistemological paradigms: (1) research methods should be separated from more abstract epistemological paradigms and whatever method or combination of methods seems to make sense should be employed (e.g., Reichardt & Cook, 1979), and (2) epistemological paradigms dictate research methods and, thus, combining research methods requires reconciling the competing positivistic and interpretive paradigms (e.g., Smith 1983a, 1983b).

This creates a dilemma. Reichardt and Cook (1979) offered good arguments in support of combining quantitative and qualitative methods, but their general suggestion that the two paradigms of research are logically independent of the methods of obtaining knowledge was a heavy price to pay. On the other hand, Smith (1983b) was correct to require a logical connection between paradigms and research methods. By tracing the implications of the positivist versus interpretive paradigms, however, he drew the unwelcome conclusion that qualitative and quantitative methods "do not seem compatible" (p. 12).

This dilemma should have been a non-starter, for it was based on the moribund positivist paradigm. It was taken seriously because the traditional educational research community was steeped in quantitative methods, and therefore resisted the perceived *unscientific* features of qualitative methods.

Quantitative and Qualitative Data

The most frequent positivist-inspired charge against qualitative data was that it is "subjective." Scriven (1972) responded that "subjective" is ambiguous and that trading on this ambiguity leads to erroneous conclusions about the merit of qualitative methods. He distinguished between "quantitative" and "qualitative" subjectivity. To say that a claim is "quantitatively" subjective means that it is based on the judgments of relatively few individuals; to say a claim is "qualitatively" subjective means that it is based on judgments that are not intersubjectively testable. Scriven's crucial point was that a claim that is subjective in one of these senses is not necessarily subjective in the other sense. For example, at one time the claim "The earth is spherical" was quantitatively subjective, but it is (and never was) qualitatively subjective because it can (could) be tested in terms of evidence and reasoning. On the other hand, "Chocolate ice cream tastes better than rocky road" is qualitatively but (probably) not quantitatively subjective. Although many would assent to this claim, it is inappropriate (and unimportant) to try to establish whether it is correct.

Scriven's (1972) distinction was useful because it helped remove one common source of confusion. But the real issue for educational research is fallibility. To disparage the subjectivity of qualitative data subjective is to label it as highly fallible; to laud the objectivity of quantitative data is to label it as minimally fallible.

For the positivists, the least fallible empirical claims—and the building blocks of scientific knowledge—were embodied in theory-neutral observation sentences. Protracted efforts, however, to produce a satisfactory explication of the relationship between such observation sentences and scientific theories (which, if successful, would have met the positivists' goal of reducing theory to a logical concatenation of observation sentences) met with failure. The line of demarcation between theory and observations grew ever more blurred and gave way to the notion that all observation is theory-laden.

Quine (1969) provides the best post-positivist account of observation sentences (exemplars of the least fallible empirical claims) . Although his characterization does not meet the demands of the positivists, he claims it "accords with the traditional role of the observation sentence as the court of appeal of scientific theories" (p. 87). He explains,

> An observation sentence is one to which all speakers of the language give the same verdict when given the concurrent stimulation. To put the point negatively, an observation sentence is one that is not sensitive to differences in past experiences within the speech community. (pp. 86-87)

Note three things about this definition. First, in the positive formulation, observations are based on the criterion of intersubjective agreement among observers and, accordingly, they always retain some degree of fallibility because the need for conceptual revision—or "paradigm shifts," to use Kuhnian language (1962)—loom as a possibility. Second, in the negative formulation, observation sentences are objective (or unbiased) in that they do not depend on irrelevant idiosyncrasies of observers. Third, neither the positive nor the negative formulation requires observation sentences to be *neutral* in the sense of being independent of speech communities associated with various paradigms, theories, or conceptual schemes. On the contrary, the relation of observation sentences to speech communities is what distinguishes Quine's view (as well as Kuhn's and many other post-positivistic philosophers' views) from the positivists'.

Abandoning the rigid positivist distinction between observation and theory in favor of a view like Quine's provides a useful perspective on the debate over quantitative versus qualitative data. At first glance, quantitative data might appear to be uniformly superior. The claim "There are x students in the classroom" is one of Quine's observation sentences, and the data are low in fallibility (i.e., intersubjective agreement will be high and different backgrounds of observers will not play a role). By contrast, observing the workings of a classroom in terms of the group dynamics results in qualitative data far removed from observation sentences, and the data are high in fallibility (i.e., intersubjective agreement will not be high and different backgrounds of observers will play a role). Given this comparison, quantitative data are much less fallible than qualitative data; and such comparisons no doubt account for the tremendous faith often placed in quantitative data. The essential point is that this case cannot be generalized; just the opposite ordering of fallibility between quantitative and qualitative data is possible and, indeed, common.

For example, consider pilot testing an opinion survey instrument. The ultimate aim of developing such an instrument is to gather quantitative data, but experience teaches that opinion surveys frequently suffer from difficulties in interpretation that may render data of questionable validity. In other words, without concerted development efforts, opinion surveys tend to be highly fallible relative to the questions of interest. What is the solution? It is to assemble some respondents, give them provisional versions of the instrument, and request their interpretations. Because their interpretations constitute qualitative data, qualitative data function to reduce the fallibility of the quantitative data to be ultimately collected. In this case, the qualitative data are presumed to be less fallible than ungrounded quantitative data. Judgments about the validity of measurement often have the characteristic of being supported by qualitative data and judgment. Thus, quantitative data often "presume" qualitative data (Campbell, 1974, 1979).

Behaviorism constitutes the most important historical challenge to the view on qualitative data so far advanced. Crudely put, behaviorism attempts to ground psychology in the "objectively observable" by eliminating all reference to nonobservables, for example, agents' intentions. Strongly influenced by positivism, behaviorists sought to mimic the methodology of physics (which ironically the positivists totally misrepresented). Not surprisingly, the behaviorists' project failed, both practically and theoretically. On the one hand, the attempt at "thin" description, as it were, proved impracticable (MacKenzie, 1977). On the other hand, behaviorism's positivist methodological constraint that categorically bars qualitative data (particularly in the form of subjects' self-reports) involved a fundamental philosophical flaw.

The elimination of all reference to the unobservable and mental—the elimination of things such as reasons, motives, and intentions in explanations of human behavior—is philosophically flawed because it obliterates the distinction between "actions" on the one hand and mere "bodily movements" on the other (Melden, 1966). This renders it impossible to distinguish, for instance, the *movement* of a person's arm rising (e.g., by reflex) and the *action* of purposively raising one's arm (e.g., to ask a question). Less drastic, but more likely to create problems in educational research, the elimination of intentions also obliterates the distinction between different actions that are associated with the same movements. For example, failing to make eye contact when being spoken to can indicate defiance (the interpretation for middle class American children) or respect (the interpretation for Latino children). This difference can be captured only by appeal to intentions because the movement (looking askance) is the same in each case.

Behaviorists have tended to be unimpressed with philosophical considerations about mental concepts. They charge that attributing intentions is subjective and unscientific, and they make much of the fact that attributing intentions often depends on self-reports. Rushton (1982) gives the example of a defendant's testimony in a criminal trial as evidence for the untrustworthiness of reports about intentions. Ironically, the doubt about the report in this case depends on belief about the existence of another intention, namely, the intention to avoid punishment. Moreover, a point often missed is that the defendant's intentions have explanatory and predictive value. If, for instance, it turns out that a piece of overt behavior is self defense and not murder, then one can predict that releasing the accused will not lead to harm to innocent members of society.

The notion that attributions of intentions must be highly fallible is part of positivist dogma. Behaviorists serve an unbalanced diet of examples, cooked up to make their point. There is often little reason to doubt the connection among agents' reports, intentions, and behavior. As Wilson (1967) observes,

> I can be certain that Churchill did not intend to give in to Hitler and I can be certain that the reason why my wife went to town yesterday was to buy a hat-not because of any scientific procedure, but (briefly) because they said so and there is no reason to suppose them insincere; moreover, their behavior gives me supporting reasons for what their intentions were. (p. 210)

Even granting that attributions of intention are less reliable than identifications of overt behavior, it does not follow that intentions should be eschewed; this would be succumbing to the "tyranny of reliability" (Messick, 1981). Increased reliability does not by itself reduce fallibility regarding the question of interest. In this connection, Taylor (1964) observes that behaviorists and near behaviorists face a dilemma: they are either saddled with an intention-free (even if highly reliable) set of constructs that is too descriptively impoverished to capture the complexity of human behavior, or they must surreptitiously incorporate intentions and qualitative means of investigating them (see also Mackenzie, 1977).

The nature of concepts used in educational research—concepts like intelligence, reasoning, achievement, and attitude—is such that dependence on qualitative judgments and data is required to minimize the fallibility of quantitative instruments. So long as educational research remains couched in terms of such concepts (and it must to have a bearing on practice), quantitative data gathering will have to remain faithful to and parasitic on qualitative judgments.

Scientific Inference

Whether quantitative or qualitative, data are used to support inferences; the way the positivists construed scientific inference in particular contributes markedly to posing the forced choice between the positivist and interpretivist paradigms of social research methodology.

The positivists' general view of scientific inference has two important features: (a) scientific inference consists of confirming (disconfirming) quantitative theories and laws by appeal to their logically inferred observational consequences, and (b) the logic of scientific inference is (or ought to be) the same for social science as for physical science. If the positivists' position is correct, then quantitative and qualitative methods are indeed incompatible and we are forced to choose between them. But both of the positivists' claims about scientific inference are mistaken.

Inference in Physical Science

Post-positivist philosophy of science[3] rejects the notion that the relationship between empirical evidence and corresponding laws and theories is a precise one, explicable in terms of formal logic. The post-positivist (Quineian-Kuhnian) view is roughly as follows: One begins with a hypothesis that is tested against evidence deemed appropriate. The evidence will either provisionally confirm the hypothesis or prove inconsistent with it. In the latter case, the evidence may either be discounted (e.g., attributed to a poor reading of the results, or inaccurate measurement, or simply viewed as anomalous), or it may be accepted as falsifying. If it is accepted as falsifying, then matters become complicated because the empirical test does not apply to the hypothesis in isolation, but to a constellation of beliefs (a "conceptual scheme" or "paradigm") in which the hypothesis is embedded. In effect, a conjunction of beliefs, including the hypothesis of interest, is put to the test. When evidence is accepted as falsifying, some further choice must be made regarding which belief in the conjunction is affected, and this decision cannot simply be read off from the evidence provided by the empirical test. In addition to the evidence from given empirical tests, other empirical beliefs, metaphysical beliefs, and general guiding principles such as simplicity, scope, and familiarity come into play in deciding how the evidence should affect the shape of the revised conceptual scheme (Quine, 1970).

In the physical sciences, quantified laws are employed that significantly circumscribe the area of interest and what is to count as confirming and disconfirming evidence. Nonetheless, the post-positivist viewpoint entails that quantitative evidence, even in the physical sciences, can never be interpreted independent of extra-observational and extra-theoretical (qualitative) considerations that help define both the theory in question and the broader conceptual scheme in which the theory is embedded; quantification does not eliminate qualitative judgments and therefore is not an *alternative* to them.

Inference in Social Research

The purpose of social research is (or ought to be) to improve human practices, and this counts against the second feature of the positivistic construal of scientific inference: that the same characterization of inference that applies to physical science also applies to social science. If social research is to inform constructive change, the concepts it employs must be validated in terms of human interests and practices.[4] Because quantitative data must be grounded in such concepts, only modest networks of quantitative laws are possible; concepts like "reasoning," "achievement," and "attitude" do not readily lend themselves to relationships like $f=ma$.[5] Inferences based on quantitative social science data are therefore much more piecemeal and disjointed than inferences in physical science, which is to say they require extra-theoretical (or qualitative) judgment to a dramatically higher degree.[6]

Although the fit between hypotheses, empirical tests associated with them, and resultant data is much looser in social research than in physics, there is no incoherence in employing quantitative methods. Even in the physical sciences, where the aim is quantitative law-building, quantitative findings do not dictate all of the scientific judgments that have to be made. As already stated, various assumptions and beliefs within both a theory itself and the broader conceptual scheme in which the theory is embedded invariably come into play.

Dogma 2: The Fact/Value Dichotomy

In response to the "value-free doctrine," Michael Scriven remarks,

... attacking the value-free doctrine accurately and effectively is important because there are so many spurious reasons for adopting it and so much value-phobic pressure to accept it . . . if the doctrine is not rendered completely absurd by complete exposure, it will simply continue to rise from the ashes. (1983, P. 81)

Against Scriven's view, value-freedom and the associated rigid fact/value dichotomy are urged on two grounds: positivist epistemology and the desire to avoid value bias. Each of these justifications is vulnerable to post-positivist criticisms. Because Donald Campbell (1982) articulates both reasons, his views may serve as a foil.

The Epistemological Justification for the Fact/Value Dichotomy

By his own admission, Campbell (1982) follows the logical positivists on the fact/value dichotomy. His basic epistemological stance is contained in the following:

The tools of descriptive science and formal logic can help us implement values which we already accept or have chosen, but they are not constitutive of those values. Ultimate values are accepted but not justified. (p. 123)

The claim that ultimate values "are accepted but not justified" is true, but this observation is not unique to values. The contrast between values and the "tools of descriptive science and formal logic" is not one that Campbell can consistently make. Elsewhere, Campbell (1974) argues for the "presumptive" nature of scientific knowledge. That is, he shares the general Kuhnian view that knowledge is based on theory-laden observations and beliefs. The consequence of construing knowledge as presumptive is that there can be no ultimate justification for beliefs of any kind, including basic scientific ones. Thus, Campbell's way of distinguishing factual and value claims—on the basis of whether they must be "accepted but not justified"—fails.

The positivist fact/value dichotomy was, after all, based on positivism's central (and contra-Kuhnian) notion that neutral observational knowledge could be isolated and used as the basis for theory. To qualify as a legitimate knowledge claim, to be "cognitively significant," a claim had to be testable either in terms of direct observation or in terms of formal logic. (Notice the similarity to Campbell's "tools of descriptive science and formal logic.") Because value claims could not be verified (or falsified) in either of these ways, they were judged to be devoid of cognitive content. An often overlooked but crucially important implication of the abandonment of positivism is this: the positivist construal of the fact/value distinction is merely a corollary of the more general theory/observation distinction. If the positivistic attempt to ground all knowledge in some sort of atheoretical reality is untenable, then so is the deep divide between facts and values.

Accordingly, it is misguided to attempt to separate value judgments from the conduct of social research on the grounds that values are noncognitive. In his discussion of post-positivist social science, Scriven (1969) puts the matter as follows:

> There is no "ultimate observation language . . . " Analogously, there is no ultimate factual language. And the more interesting side of this coin is that many statements which in one context clearly would be evaluational are, in another, clearly factual. Obvious examples include judgments of intelligence and of the merit of performances such as those of runners of the Olympic Games. (p. 199)

Scriven concludes, ". . . there is no possibility that the social sciences can be free either of value claims in general or of moral value claims in particular. . ." (p. 201). Rorty (1982b) echoes and extends Scriven's position:

> . . . there is no way to prevent anybody using *any* term "evaluatively." If you ask some-body whether he is using "repression" or "primitive" or "working class" normatively or descriptively, he might be able to answer in the case of a given statement, made on a given occasion. But if you ask him whether he uses the term only when he is describing, only when he is engaging in moral reflection, or both, the answer is almost always going to be "both." Further—and this is the crucial point—unless the answer is "both," it is not the sort of term that will do us much good in social science. (pp. 195–196)

The view exemplified by Scriven and Rorty holds that social science concepts are neither descriptive nor evaluative per se, but are two-edged—the distinction between description and evaluation depends on the contexts in which concepts occur. Value judgments may not be excluded from the arena of rational criticism in general or from the conduct of research in particular. No researcher, whatever the field, can avoid value commitments (whether or not such commitments are acknowledged). It is absurd, for example, to suggest that the physicists participating in the Manhattan Project to develop nuclear weapons were engaged in a value-free enterprise. It is even more absurd to suggest that social research can be value-free because social research is *doubly value-laden*. Not only is social research circumscribed by values that determine things such as funding and how research results should be used; as Scriven and Rorty observe, the very concepts social researchers employ are evaluative of human behavior.

Avoiding Bias

An epistemological justification for the fact/value dichotomy went the way of positivism, but the distinction persists—rises from the ashes as Scriven says—as the result of well intentioned but misguided efforts to avoid bias. For example, consider the motives Campbell (1982) exhibits in the following:

> An established power structure with the ability to employ applied social scientists, the machinery of social science, and control over the means of dissemination produces an unfair status quo bias in the mass production of belief assertions from the applied social sciences . . . . This state of affairs is one which . . . I deplore, but I find myself best able to express my disapproval through retaining the old-fashioned construct of truth, warnings against individually and clique selfish distortions, and a vigorously exhorted fact/value distinction . . . . (p. 125)

[The] effort to make us aware of biased-paradigm co-optation is again one best done by retaining a traditional fact/value distinction; it is a matter of becoming self-critically aware of our profoundly relativistic epistemological predicament and using this awareness in the service of a more competent effort to achieve objectivity, rather than employing it to justify giving up the goal of truth. (p. 126)

Campbell clearly opposes the manipulation of social scientific knowledge in a way that serves the interests of powerful groups—a laudable position. By waving the banner of value-free social science, however, Campbell is more likely contributing to than avoiding bias. To illustrate the danger, consider the concept of intelligence and whether it is possible to strictly separate truth, facts, and values. If research on intelligence involves solely the "goal of truth," it should be possible to divest it of evaluative meaning. Is this possible? The furor generated by research into different mean intelligence test scores across ethnic and cultural groups indicates that intelligence is not in fact value-free (see, e.g., Goodnow, 1984). Ordering groups in terms of intelligence implicitly evaluates those at the top as better.

Furthermore, "intelligence" cannot be rendered value-free and retain its present interest. Perverse policy recommendations and shoddy testing practices notwithstanding, it is precisely because intelligence is associated with an array of valued capabilities and activities that it is a useful social science concept. Unlike "velocity" *qua* physical science concept, "intelligence" *qua* social science concept would be uninteresting if it were not associated with valued human practices and goals. Research on intelligence under the banner of value-freedom is dangerous because it introduces (not eliminates) the potential for bias—and not merely the kind of bias involved in the outrage of administering intelligence tests to those not fluent in the language of the test. Intelligence tests measure characteristics that are implicitly viewed as valuable and therefore introduce the possibility of a more fundamental kind of bias. It is not too hard to imagine a society in which I.Q. tests would measure the ability to construct a bark canoe. Closer to home, just as the label "intelligent" entails roughly "having something good," the label "mentally retarded" entails roughly "lacking something good." Consider the well-known effects of labeling school children on the criterion of intelligence (and on numerous other criteria as well).

Value judgments are built into the vocabulary social research employs and the purpose it serves. The problem with Campbell's (1982) "vigorously exhorted fact/value distinction" is the implication that issues of value can (and should) be set to one side while researchers go about the task of collecting purely descriptive data. At an epistemological level, because social science concepts are inherently evaluative, it is impossible within social research to systematically divest factual claims of their evaluative dimensions. At the level of practice, the attempt to bracket values in the name of truth and science in order to avoid bias only results in an insidious form of bias.

If value judgments are irrevocably noncognitive, or biased, or to be "accepted but not justified," then social research must be flawed in the same way. This conclusion can be avoided by accepting that value judgments are part of the fabric of social research and recognizing that value judgments must be defended and may be criticized like any other kind of judgment. As Scriven (1983) says,

> Value judgments, like factual judgments and theoretical analyses, are of two kinds-the well supported and the poorly supported. No scientist can avoid making them, although it is certainly possible to avoid making good ones. (p. 81)

Conclusion: Toward Closing the Old Divides

Educational research freed of positivist dogmas has two general characteristics. First, procrustean standards of criticism based on the quantitative/qualitative dogma are eschewed. The merit of a given research project depends on how it responds to the fallibility of the question at issue, the fallibility of relevant background beliefs, the nature of the question, and the broad practical and ethical constraints under which the investigation must be conducted. Although it often makes sense to emphasize quantitative methods to the exclusion of qualitative methods or vice versa, there are no mechanical rules for making these decisions and no good reasons to avoid combining methods. The only generally applicable criterion is whether, all things considered, there are good reasons to doubt what the researcher claims to have found. Criticisms that the researcher failed to randomize or failed to capture the insider's perspective have no force when divorced from particular studies.

Second, values should not be bracketed or submerged; value issues are ubiquitous and value judgments must be rationally justified.[7] Studies are subject to criticism on the basis of moral considerations *internal* to the conduct of research (e.g., obtaining informed consent from subjects, and being cognizant of the possible effects of value-laden terms). Studies are also subject to criticism on the basis of social utility considerations *external* to the conduct of research (e.g., the worth of the knowledge obtained). The legitimacy of criticism in terms of social utility implies that educational research should be consciously linked to critically assessed educational aims rather than being limited to working out the minutiae of the latest line of research. As Wilson (1983) observes,

> Education . . . [is] . . . shot through and through with the necessity of making value judgments . . . . If we do not get the concepts and categories clear in the first place, we shall not know what or what sort of facts, theories, and practices we ought to look at. (p. 192)

Bracketing or submerging questions of values in the design or conduct of educational research greatly increases the probability of three undesirable outcomes. First, such value-free research can be useless. If no link exists between research and practical concerns, the research will have no ability to improve practice. Second, such value-free research can be inefficient. If a belated, ad hoc, partial link is established between research and practical concerns, energy and resources will have been wasted. Finally, such value-free research can be dangerous. Because no research can really be value-free, bracketing or submerging values can have insidious effects.

Notes

1 The analytic/synthetic distinction (the first "dogma" or central tenet) was crucial in logical positivism. Synthetic statements were defined as ones whose truth-value could be determined solely by appeal to observation (e.g., Grass is green). Analytic statements were defined as ones whose truth-value could be determined solely by appeal to logic and meanings (e.g., All bachelors are unmarried). Any statement that was to count as "cognitively significant" (i.e., legitimate in science) had to be verifiable either in terms of observation (if it were synthetic) or in terms of logic and meanings (if it were analytic). All other statements were barred. The class of illegitimate statements included "metaphysical" ones (e.g., "God exists") and "emotive" ones (e.g., "Abortion is morally wrong"). Quine(1962) attacked the analytic/synthetic distinction directly and convincingly and showed that verificationism (the second "dogma" or central tenet) is, at bottom, identical to the analytic-synthetic "dogma." In the process, he paved the way for the kind of post-positivistic interpretation of science made prominent by Kuhn in which all scientific knowledge is seen to be theory-laden and not neatly divisible into the purely observational (or synthetic) and the purely theoretical (or analytic).

2 "Logical positivism" and "positivism" are used loosely in this chapter. Logical positivism, strictly speaking, died as the result of insuperable internal difficulties prior to the appearance of Quine's paper (Passmore, 1967). Quine undermined the attenuated form of logical positivism frequently referred to as "logical empiricism."

3 By "post-positivism" I mean the term literally, to be distinguished from "neo-positivism."

4 The much-lamented gap between theory and practice is partially attributable to the vocabularies social researchers choose. Rorty (1982b) sets down two requirements for the vocabulary of social science: (1) it should contain descriptions of situations that facilitate their prediction and control, and (2) it should contain descriptions that help one decide what to do (p. 197). Preoccupation with the first requirement eliminates attention to the second, and this reverses priorities. Given that the aim is to improve practice, ensuring that concepts employed are useful toward this end is paramount. The charge that such concepts are unscientific and value-laden is an objection only if the question of purposes is begged.

5 Toulmin (1953), for example, argues that physicists are free to invent vocabularies and a well-behaved mathematical system to suit their aim of investigating "the form of given regularities." By contrast, "natural historians" (which presumably includes social scientists) must use a less technical and public vocabulary fitted to their aim of investigating "regularities of given forms" (p. 53).

6 Notably, this is consistent with Kuhn's remarks about social research. Despite the manner in which his notion of a "paradigm" (Kuhn, 1962) has caught fire among educational researchers and has been used to contrast quantitative and qualitative methods, he excluded social science (let alone individual methods) on the grounds that it has never had an accepted core of theory required to constitute a "scientific paradigm" or to make for "scientific revolutions."

7 For excellent discussions of how ethical theorizing is cognitive and may be construed in a way analogous to the post-positivist, presumptive view of scientific theorizing, see Daniels (1979) and Werner (1983).

Chapter 3

THE QUANTITATIVE QUALITATIVE DOGMA, THE INCOMPATIBILITY THESIS, AND THE PRAGMATIC ALTERNATIVE

Combining quantitative and qualitative methods has become commonplace in educational research. Indeed, such a combination is not only permitted, but often encouraged. But this methodological innovation was not without its detractors. Advocates of what I call the "incompatibility thesis" criticized it on the grounds that the alleged compatibility between quantitative and qualitative methods is merely apparent; the idea that quantitative and qualitative methods may be combined ignores deep epistemological difficulties and ultimately rests on the epistemologically suspect criterion of "what works" (e.g., Guba, 1987; Smith 1983a, 1983b; Smith & Heshusius, 1986).

The incompatibility thesis permits *disjunctive* combinations of quantitative and qualitative methods within the same study, in which different methods are applied to different questions but in which the study as a whole presupposes different epistemological paradigms. The incompatibility thesis bars *conjunctive* combinations of methods, in which different methods may be applied to the same questions and in which the study as a whole presupposes the same epistemological paradigm.

This chapter advances the alternative "compatibility thesis," the view that a thoroughgoing integration of quantitative and qualitative methods is advisable and involves no epistemological incoherence. It has four major sections.

I begin by briefly illustrating how, in practice, differences between quantitative and qualitative data, design, analysis, and interpretation can be accounted for largely in terms of differences in research interests and judgments about how best to pursue them. That differences can be accounted for in these ways should prompt suspicion about the need to posit different and incompatible epistemological paradigms to account for the use of different research methods.

This initial suspicion sets the stage for the second section. Incompatibilists maintain that problems are largely hidden at the level of methods, and become clearly visible only at the level of epistemological paradigms. In particular, they advance an argument along the following lines: (1) Positivist and interpretivist paradigms underlie quantitative and qualitative methods, respectively; (2) the two kinds of paradigms are incompatible; therefore, (3) the two kinds of methods are incompatible. I argue that a principle implicit in the incompatibilist's argument— that abstract paradigms should determine research methods in a one-way fashion—is untenable and advance an alternative, pragmatic view: that paradigms must demonstrate their worth in terms of how they inform, *and are informed by*, research methods that are successfully employed. Given such a two-way relationship between research methods and epistemological paradigms, they must be evaluated in terms of how well they can be brought into equillibrium.

In the third section, I characterize and discuss five general standards for evaluating educational research (adapted from Howe & Eisenhart, 1990). These standards are specifically formulated to be consistent with the compatibility thesis, for they apply indifferently to both quantitative and qualitative research.

Finally, I consider several criticisms that are commonly advanced against the pragmatic philosophical stance that underlies compatibilism. Specifically, pragmatism rejects epistemological imperatives that cannot be squared with the actual practices employed in gaining empirical knowledge. As a consequence, pragmatism is often accused of holding truth hostage to "what works" and of therefore being committed to relativism and irrationalism. I suggest that the threat of relativism and irrationalism purportedly posed by pragmatism is overdrawn, if not based on an outright misrepresentation of the pragmatic view, and that the alternative views of truth associated with the incompatibility thesis have serious problems of their own.

The Incompatibility Thesis and Research Practice

Consider Phillip Jackson's remarks regarding his pioneering "qualitative" educational research:

> Classroom life, in my judgment, is too complex an affair to be viewed or talked about from any single perspective. Accordingly, as we try to grasp the meaning of what school is like for students and teachers we must not hesitate to use all the ways of knowing at our disposal. This means we must read, and look, and listen, and count things, and talk to people, and even muse introspectively over the memories of our own childhood. (1968, pp. vii- viii)

Now, consider Michael Huberman's remarks:

> [In] any study, there are only bits and pieces that can be legitimated on "scientific" grounds. The bulk comes from common sense, from prior experience, from the logic inherent in the problem definition or the problem space. Take the review of the literature, the conceptual model, the key variables, the measures, and so forth, and you have perhaps 20% of what is really going into your study.... And if you look hard at that 20%, if for example, you go back to the prior studies from which you derived many assumptions and

perhaps some measures, you will find that they, too, are 20% topsoil and 80% landfill. (Huberman, 1987, p. 12)

Huberman's remarks came some twenty years later than Jackson's, after the quantitative/qualitative debate was in full swing. Despite the growing concerns about the incompatibility of quantitative and qualitative research methods, Jackson and Huberman make a quite similar point: the practice of educational research is pervasively and unavoidably dependent on background knowledge and the exercise of practical judgment.

In this section, I apply this observation to three basic components of Research: data, design and analysis, and interpretation of results. My primary aims are to show that the quantitative/qualitative distinction is not pivotal within a larger scheme of background knowledge and practical research purposes, and that the incompatibility thesis does not accurately characterize the real problems that confront educational researchers as they carry out their investigations.

Data

When applied to data, the quantitative/qualitative distinction is ambiguous between its traditional meaning in measurement and the "intentionalist" meaning it has taken on because of its association with "qualitative" research methods. In terms of the measurement meaning, data are qualitative if they fit a categorical measurement scale; data are quantitative if they fit an ordinal, interval, or ratio scale. In terms of the intentionalist meaning, data are qualitative if they incorporate norms, values, beliefs, and intentions that go with the "insider's perspective;" data are quantitative (and here some extrapolation is required) if they exclude norms, values, beliefs, and intentions that go with the insider's perspective.

Combining these two meanings of qualitative and quantitative data yields four types (or potential types) of data, examples of which are provided in Table 3.1. The question to be asked of the incompatibility thesis is: In what way(s) are these types of data incompatible with one another?

Incompatibilists would be hard pressed to show that the problem exists between the rows (i.e., with the measurement meaning). This would entail that researchers cannot mix variables that are on different measurement scales, which is absurd. Perhaps the incompatibility is to be found between the columns (i.e., with the intentionalist meaning). But this sort of incompatibility seems equally difficult to defend, for the implication would be that it is illicit to mix demographic variables such as income with behavioral variables such as moral reasoning skills. This would condemn much, if not most, educational research as incoherent.

The remaining option for the incompatibilist is to bar one or more of the cells (i.e., to locate incompatibility in certain combinations of the measurement and intentionalist meanings). The most suspect cell is III, in which moral reasoning

Table 3.1. Four types of qualitative/quantitative

		Intentionalist Meaning	
		Qualitative	Quantitative
Measurement Meaning	Qualitative	I Moral Reasoning	II Poverty Level
	Quantitative	III Moral Reasoning in Terms of Kohlbergian Stages	IV Income in Dollars

(a qualitative concept in terms of intentional meaning) is put on an ordinal (i.e., quantitative) measurement scale.

A prominent view is that quantification *objectifies* concepts and thereby divests them of their intentionalist dimensions. But by what sort of magic does this occur? Does changing from a pass-fail to an A-F grading scale, for instance, imply that some radically different kind of performance is being described and evaluated? If not, then why should the case be different when researchers move from speaking of things like moral reasoning in terms of present and absent, high and low, or good and bad to speaking of them in terms of Stage 1 to Stage 6?

That many *believe* that quantification objectifies—on both sides of the quantitative/qualitative divide—is an important part of the quantitative/qualitative dogma. But this belief is based on a confusion encouraged by the ambiguity of "quantitative" versus "qualitative." To be sure, quantification often diminishes the capacity to capture nuance and context. But whether to accept this disadvantage is tied to judgments about whether it is outweighed by the advantage of gathering data that, among other things, permits precise comparisons. This practical judgment is as deep as the issue goes.

As I argued in the previous chapter, the vocabulary of social research, or at least a good portion of it, is two-edged, both descriptive (or quantitative in the intentionalist sense) and evaluative (or qualitative in the intentionalist sense). The concept of moral reasoning is good example. Quantifying it does not divest of its intentionalist (particularly evaluative) dimensions. It may well hide them from view (an issues discussed in Chapter 2 in terms of intelligence); and, of course, the ordering from low to high, or less adequate to more adequate, or whatever, may also be highly controversial (as Gilligan's critique of Kohlberg's hierarchy clearly shows). These are serious problems, to be sure, but they do not find their source in the alleged incompatibility between qualitative and quantitative data.

Design and Analysis

The quantitative/qualitative distinction is at once most accurately and most deceptively applied at the level of design and analysis. It is accurately applied because quantitative design and analysis involve inferences that are clearly more mechanistic (i.e., nonjudgmental or "objective") and more precise than qualitative design and analysis. It is deceptively applied because quantitative design and analysis, like qualitative design and analysis, also unavoidably make numerous assumptions that are not themselves mechanistically grounded.

Using "design" loosely, the qualitative researcher's design consists of some provisional questions to investigate, some data collection sites, and a schedule allocating time for data collection, analysis (typically ongoing), and writing up results. The quantitative researcher's design also has these elements, but the questions are more precisely and exhaustively stated and the schedule more sharply distinguishes the data collection, analysis, and write-up phases of the research. Furthermore, the quantitative researcher will have clearly specified the research design (in a more strict sense) and the statistical analysis procedures to be employed.

The differences between these two researchers turns on, or at least ought to turn on, what each is attempting to investigate and what assumptions each is willing to make. That is, the qualitative researcher (rightly or wrongly) is willing to assume relatively little, to keep the investigation open-ended and sensitive to unanticipated features of the object of study. The qualitative researcher is also acutely sensitive to the particulars of the context, especially the descriptions and explanations of events supplied by actors involved. In contrast, the quantitative researcher (rightly or wrongly) is willing to assume much, e.g., that all confounding variables have been identified and that the variables of interest can be validly measured; quantitative researchers are also much less interested in actors' points of view.

The chief differences between quantitative and qualitative designs and analysis can be accounted for in terms of the questions of interest and their place within a complex web of background knowledge. Because quantitative research circumscribes the variables of interest, measures them in prescribed ways, and specifies the relationships among them that are to be investigated, quantitative data analysis has a mechanistic, non-judgmental component in the form of statistical inference. But, as Huberman (1987) notes, this component is small in the overall execution of a given research project, and it is far too easy to overestimate the degree to which quantitative studies, by virtue of employing precise measurement and statistics, are eminently "objective" and "scientific." One gets to the point of employing statistical tests only by first making numerous judgments about what counts as a valid measure of the variables of interest, what variables threaten to confound comparisons, and what statistical tests are appropriate. Accordingly, the results of a given statistical analysis are only as credible as their background assumptions and arguments, and these are not amenable to mechanistic demonstration. Furthermore, even highly quantitative studies require that the context be made intelligible by use of some sort of narrative ("qualitative") history of events (e.g., Campbell, 1979).

Interpretation of Results

The distinction between data analysis and interpretation of results is an admittedly artificial one, especially for qualitative research, but quantitative researchers by no means proceed in a lockstep fashion regarding interpretation either. As studies enter the analysis and interpretation phases, quantitative researchers look for new confounds, new relationships, new ways of aggregating and coding data, etc., not envisioned in the original design. Except for being hemmed in by earlier decisions about what to measure and how to measure it, they look a lot like qualitative researchers. Both kinds of researchers construct arguments based on their evidence, ever wary of alternative interpretations of their data.

Actual studies invariably mix kinds of interpretation, and whether a given study is dubbed "quantitative" or "qualitative" is a matter of emphasis. For instance, Coleman's (1968) work on equal opportunity fits the description "quantitative" despite his extended "qualitative" concern over just what his data meant with respect to the concept "equal educational opportunity." Conversely, Jackson's (1968) investigation of classroom life fits the description "qualitative" despite his modest use of "quantitative" methods.

The Incompatibility Thesis and Epistemological Paradigms

Are there deeper epistemological reasons, to which research practitioners are blind, for avoiding the combination of quantitative and qualitative methods?

Incompatibilists might very well grant the general thrust of the preceding section by responding that compatibility is possible with respect to "techniques and procedures" (Smith & Heshusius, 1986) or the "methods level" (Guba, 1987). They contend, however, that this is only a misleading surface compatibility and that at a deeper epistemological level—at "the logic of justification" or "paradigm" level—quantitative and qualitative methods are indeed incompatible because of the different conceptions of reality, truth, the relationship between the investigator and the object of investigation, and so forth, that each assumes. As Guba puts it, "The one [paradigm] precludes the other just as surely as belief in a round world precludes belief in a flat one" (p. 31).

The incompatibility thesis (briefly described earlier) will now be more fully fleshed out. (Henceforth "paradigm" and "methods" will be used to mark the distinction between the levels of epistemology and research practice, respectively.)

The incompatibility thesis distinguishes two epistemological paradigms. One paradigm is positivism: the view that scientific knowledge is the paragon of rationality; that scientific knowledge must be free of *metaphysics*, that is, that it must be based on *neutral* observation that is free of the interests, values, purposes, and psychological schemata of individuals; and that anything that deserves the name "knowledge," including social science, of course, must measure up to these standards. The other paradigm is interpretivism: the view that, at least as far as the social sciences are concerned, metaphysics (in the form of human intentions, beliefs, and so forth) cannot be eliminated; observation cannot be neutral in the sense of altogether excluding interests, values, purposes, and psychological schemata; and investigation must aim for interpretive understanding (as opposed to the aims of explanation, prediction, and control that characterize the positivistic paradigm). These differences render the positivist and interpretivist paradigms incompatible. Because the positivist paradigm supports quantitative methods and the interpretivist paradigm supports qualitative methods, quantitative and qualitative methods are incompatible.

There are at least two strategies that a compatibilist might employ against this thesis. First, the compatibilist can argue that the two epistemological paradigms included in the incompatibilist's argument do not exhaust the possibilities. In particular, the pragmatic tradition, which includes James, Dewey, Quine, and Kuhn and, more recently, Rorty and Bernstein, has been left entirely out of the picture.[1] This seems to be a serious omission, for pragmatists played a significant role in bringing down positivism and would clearly reject the forced choice between the interpretivist and positivist paradigms. Second, the compatibilist can take the more direct approach (also pragmatic) of insisting that paradigms bring themselves into some reasonable state of equilibrium with research methods. That is, rather than divorcing paradigms from the conduct of research (but nonetheless having them dictate what is to count as legitimate knowledge), the compatibilist can insist on a mutual adjustment between the two such that practice is neither static and unreflective nor subject to the one-way dictates of a wholly abstract epistemological paradigm.

I argued in Chapter 2 that the fall of positivism undermines the sort of forced choice between epistemological paradigms that underpins the incompatibility thesis; that is, I have already made the first gambit against the incompatibility thesis (and see Garrison, 1986). In this chapter, I focus my attention on the second.

Consider Kaplan's delightful story illustrating the "principle of the drunkard's search."

> There is a story of a drunkard searching under a street lamp for his house key, which he had dropped some distance away. Asked why he didn't look where he had dropped it, he replied, "It's lighter here!" (1964, p. 11).

Consider now the way Smith and Heshusius (1986) write off the pragmatic (compatibilist) criterion of "what works."

> In the end, what works is not a firm foundation to stand on. What works depends on the kind of work one wants inquiry to do, which in turn depends on the paradigm within which one is working. (p. 10)

The incompatibility thesis, like the drunkard's search, permits the "lights" to determine what is to be looked for and where. But why should paradigms determine the kind of work one may do with inquiry any more than the amount of illumination should determine where one may conduct a search? The possibility of modifying a paradigm in response to the demands of research seems to go unnoticed.

Eschewing this kind of "tyranny of method" (Bernstein, 1983)—of the epistemological over the practical, of the conceptual over the empirical—is the hallmark of pragmatic philosophy. Kaplan (1964) provides a particularly helpful account of this general attitude in terms of the relationship between research methods ("logic-in-use") and epistemological paradigms ("reconstructed-logic"). In particular, he contends that the two levels are intimately connected and require mutual adjustment. The following brief caricature of the rise and fall of methodological behaviorism (my example, not Kaplan's) may serve as an illustration of how this adjustment process unfolds.

Around the turn of the twentieth century, psychology was in a state of disarray. The old introspectionist logic-in-use was developing internal problems and was failing to provide useful findings. A budding behaviorist logic-in-use provided competition for dominance by making claims to being scientific and promising to yield elaborate scientific theory. To solidify its position, behaviorism turned to the reconstructed-logic provided by the positivists' analysis of natural science, and adopted that logic—with its demands for verifiability and its rejection of mental concepts and self-reports—as the methodological basis for their research. Thus, the positivistic reconstructed-logic gained preeminence, and any research methodology that failed to measure up was dismissed as unscientific.

There were pragmatic philosophers (notably, Dewey) who rejected positivism's reconstruction of science from the start. To be consistent, however, pragmatists would have had to change their view if social science based on a positivist reconstruction had "worked" at the level of a logic-in-use (though, to complicate matters, they would still have had the option of arguing for a different set of aims and values). But the positivist-inspired behaviorist social science methodology has not worked at the level of logic-in-use—it has not lived up to its promise of providing elaborate theory and has outlived the usefulness it once had (e.g., Mackenzie, 1977). Consequently, there currently is no dominant reconstructed-logic (paradigm), and many researchers have become enmeshed in questions of logic-in-use, devising whatever methods seem appropriate for investigating important questions at hand. Thus, questions about logic-in-use—nitty-gritty questions about methods—are currently leading the way; and reconstructed-logics, or epistemological paradigms, need to be brought into line.

How to frame the problem that this state of affairs engenders is where compatibilists and incompatibilists part company. One of the central concerns behind incompatibilism is legitimate: to the extent that preoccupation with methods prompts unreflectiveness and stifles progress, educational researchers ought to be pressed to take a look at deeper epistemological issues. Unfortunately, all that incompatibilism seems to have to offer is a forced choice between two exclusive epistemological paradigms and the spin-off of a fragmented research community—with one group championing the view that their method is the only truly "scientific" one (a view that may be associated with certain hard-headed positivist types), and the other group embracing "multiple realities" so that researchers are free to speak their own languages, investigate their own questions, and come up with their own standards of truth (a view that may be associated with certain soft-headed interpretivist types). Neither dogmatic adherence to the positivistic pipe dream nor chaotic methodological relativism (let alone the two, side by side) promise to advance educational research.

The way out of this dilemma is to give up the notion that social research must be either *just like* physical science or *fundamentally different* from it. The incompatibility thesis ignores this possibility because, to borrow again from Kaplan (1964), it confuses "two things to understand" (intentionalist and non-intentionalist) with "two kinds of understanding" (scientific and interpretive). The compatibilist view admits that social research needs to use a vocabulary appropriate for describing social events, which means using intentionalist concepts. Compatibilism admits as well that physics has no need for such concepts. Unlike the subjects of social research, the objects of physical research cannot question the way researchers choose to describe them, provide their own accounts of why events happened as they did, or alter their behavior in response to researchers' claims. Compatibilism thereby grants something to the interpretivist paradigm regarding the special nature of social research.

On the other hand, compatibilism denies that it is incoherent to quantify intentionalist concepts, to employ non-intentionalist concepts, or to sometimes ignore or dismiss actors' descriptions and accounts of events. In addition, insofar as the "new philosophy of science" entails that even physics has its interpretive (non-mechanical and hermeneutical) elements (e.g., Giddens, 1976; Phillips 1987), compatibilism also denies that social research must employ any unique kind of understanding. Compatibilism thereby grants something to the positivist paradigm regarding the uniformity of scientific reasoning. By granting something to both paradigms, compatibilism thus steers a middle course that avoids running aground on either the positivist or interpretivist methodological islands.

Of course, moving beyond a forced choice between exclusive epistemological paradigms does not end the conversation about social research methodology, but it does change its focus—from *whether* combining positivist and interpretivist elements is legitimate to *how* this combination is to be accomplished.

Giddens, in his suggestively titled *New Rules of Sociological Method* (1976), contends that social research must work back and forth between the technical, scientific vocabulary of social science and the workaday, natural vocabulary of social conduct through a process he calls the "double hermeneutic." In a similar vein, Geertz (1979) argues that an understanding of human behavior requires a "continuous dialectical tacking between the most local of local detail and the most global of global structure" (p. 239). Social researchers must employ both "experience-near" concepts (thereby capturing an important element of the interpretivist paradigm) and "experience-distant" concepts (thereby capturing an important element of the positivist paradigm) to arrive at an adequate understanding:

> Confinement to experience-near concepts leaves an ethnographer awash in immediacies as well as entangled in vernacular. Confinement to experience-distant ones leaves him stranded in abstractions and smothered in jargon. The real question . . . is what kinds of roles the two kinds of concepts play in anthropological analysis. To be more exact: How, in each case, should they be deployed so as to produce an interpretation of the way people live which is neither imprisoned within their mental horizons, an ethnography of witchcraft as written by a witch, nor systematically deaf to the distinctive tonalities of witchcraft as written by a geometer? (1979, p. 227)

Notions like Geertz's "dialectical tacking" and Giddens' "double hermeneutic" suggest the outlines of the kind of compatibilist viewpoint that may supplant the incompatibilist's forced choice.

Criteria for Evaluating Educational Research

The compatibility thesis has important implications for selecting criteria for evaluating educational research. Unlike the incompatibility thesis, which requires separate criteria for quantitative and qualitative research in virtue of the features of incompatible positivist and interpretive paradigms—objectivity versus subjectivity, fixed categories versus emergent categories, the outsider's perspective versus the insider's perspective, a static reality versus a fluid reality, causal explanation versus hermeneutical understanding—the compatibility thesis requires uniform criteria to be applied across educational research. Below I briefly characterize five such uniform criteria after I first provide three observations about their general basis.

First, general standards for evaluating educational research have to be very abstract. Because educational research cuts across many disciplines and their associated methodologies, and because no one can be expected to be a master of all of the relevant disciplines, general standards have to be open with respect issues of methodology and substance peculiar to the disciplines in question. Second, notwithstanding the deference to disciplinary expertise just described, there must be some distinguishing feature(s) of educational research that make it of interest and value to educators. Third, although positivism helped spawn a set of methods (typically quantitative) such that a *vestigial methodological positivism* is still alive and well, such methods cannot and need not be justified by an appeal to positivist epistemology. Instead, such methods must, like qualitative methods, satisfy the kinds of non-positivist criteria about to be set down.

Criterion 1: The Fit Between Research Questions and Data Collection and Analysis Techniques

Hilary Putnam remarks, "If you want to know why a square peg doesn't fit into a round hole, you had better not describe the peg in terms of its constituent elementary particles" (cited in Rorty, 1982a, p. 201). Although Putnam's target is reductionism in scientific explanation, his remark also has a more prosaic meaning: the data collection techniques employed ought to fit the research question entertained. A corollary of this criterion is that research questions should drive data collection techniques and analysis rather than vice versa—and this is the form in which it is most often violated.

Correctly ordering research questions and methods is, of course, a complex issue. I do not mean to suggest that researchers can proceed as if they have super intellects—capable of competently choosing from all of the relevant questions and methodologies—nor as if they have available infinite time and resources. In some sense, then, research methodology will indeed drive research questions. But the degree to which this occurs should be minimized. It is incumbent upon educational researchers to give careful attention to the value their research questions have for informing educational practice, whether it be at the level of pedagogy, policy, or social theory, and then to formulate research designs accordingly.

Criterion 2: The Effective Application of Specific Data Collection and Analysis Techniques

In addition to coherently linking up with research questions, data collection and analysis techniques also must be competently applied, in a more or less technical sense. Various principles guide how interviews should be conducted, how instruments should be designed, how sampling should proceed, how data should be reduced, and so forth, such that rather immediate low inference conclusions are rendered credible. If credibility is not achieved at this level, then the more general (and interesting) conclusions that ultimately rest on these low inference conclusions will be suspect. As with the first criterion, I do not mean to imply that there are hard-and-fast rules that must be followed; indeed, such a stance would run counter to the major themes of this chapter.

Criterion 3: Alertness to and Coherence of Background Assumptions

Linking research questions with data collection techniques and competently applying the latter do not insure that a study will render warranted conclusions, for studies must be judged against a background of pertinent research. For example, if the results of one study contradict those of another (or several others), then some sort of explanation of why this occurred is in order. This is where the familiar review of the literature comes into play.

Whether some grand social scientific theoretical orientation is employed or research is more specifically focused on pedagogy, the ongoing problematic should help guide the research questions and methods in a coherent and consistent fashion. This is true even for research that is highly critical of and breaks with what has come before. A certain degree of continuity is required for given research to engage an area of inquiry and thus have the capacity to move it in one direction or another.

Criterion 4: Overall Warrant

As I am using the term, overall warrant encompasses responding to and balancing the first three standards as well as going beyond them, to include such things as being alert to and being able to employ knowledge from outside the particular perspective and tradition within which one is working, and being able to apply general principles for evaluating educational research. Although it is difficult (indeed wrong-headed) to try to nail down the notion of overall warrant in a much more precise way, some additional articulation is nonetheless possible.

Educational research is a "field of study" (Shulman, 1988) that draws from an array of research traditions, and its theories are in a constant state of refinement and revision. The most warranted conclusions of which researchers are capable at any given point in time are those that engage established theoretical orientations—what Denzin (1989) calls "triangulation by theory"—and that employ the most plausible one, or some modified version of it, to explain the particular research results. Such a procedure includes disconfirming as well as confirming theories (Erickson, 1982).

Criterion 5: Value Constraints

The conduct of educational research is subject to both external and internal value constraints (a point introduced in Chapter 2).

External Constraints. External value constraints have to do with the worth of research for informing and improving educational practice—the "so what?" question; that research might possess internal validity is insufficient. Although such judgments of educational worth can be very difficult to make, they are not judgments from which researchers can forever run and hide. Educational researchers should be able to communicate what value their research has (if only potentially) for educational practice and policy.

Related to this, the conclusions of educational research ought to be generally accessible to the education community. That is, the language of the results and implications must be in a form that is understandable to, and debatable by, various actors in a particular setting—teachers, administrators, parents, and also educational researchers with varying perspectives and expertise. Accordingly, the research process itself must give attention to the nature of the contexts and individuals it investigates and to which its results might be applied, that is, to their social, political, and cultural features.

Internal Constraints. Internal value constraints have to do with research ethics. I call research ethics "internal" because it has to do with the way research is conducted *vis-à-vis* research subjects, not with the (external) value of results. For example, Milgram's (1974) research on obedience to authority rendered valuable insights regarding the power of researchers to elicit compliance from subjects to perform ethically objectionable actions. The way Milgram treated his subjects was highly objectionable, however—so much so that he would not be permitted to do his research today.

Internal value constraints are distinguishable from criteria of warrant insofar as observing them sometimes requires reducing warrant. For instance, randomized double-blind experiments are notorious for the kind of trade-off they engender between the risk-benefit ratio that applies to the subjects of such research and the value of the knowledge that can be obtained for guiding future action. Especially relevant to qualitative research, researchers must weigh the quality of the data they can gather (and whether they can gather any data at all) against principles such as autonomy, privacy, and truth-telling. Although internal value constraints can be distinguished from more conventional issues of warrant, they are nonetheless clearly relevant to evaluating the validity of research designs and procedures.

Some Observations About Pragmatism

The perspective laid out in this chapter—"compatibilism"— rests heavily on an appeal to a generally pragmatic approach. It is thus likely to be dismissed on the grounds that the pragmatic criterion of "what works" is fatally flawed. The argument against the criterion is a simple one that goes like this: What worked for Newton is not what worked for Einstein, and it is absurd to say that the universe switched from being Newtonian to being Einsteinian early in the 20th century. If the universe did change its nature early in the 20th century in response to "what works" (rather than having its true nature discovered), science is irrational and relativistic. Thus, the "what works" criterion is untenable. *QED*

This attempt to dispense with pragmatism is far too facile, chiefly because pragmatists aren't about to let the distinction between "what works" and the "true nature" of things get off the ground—a point that is apparently often unappreciated (e.g., Phillips, 1983; Smith & Heshusius, 1986). The pragmatic perspective can be rendered more formidable by examining the stances toward truth, relativism, and irrationalism that pragmatists indeed hold.

Truth Is "What Works"

Pragmatists who are on their toes resist the temptation to provide a theory of truth by filling in the blank in "X is true if and only if___ " with "X works," "X is a warranted assertion," "X helps us cope," and so on (Rorty, 1982c). If they give in to this temptation, absurdity quickly results. Was the earth flat when this belief "worked"? For pragmatists, "truth" is a normative concept, like "good," and "truth is what works" is best seen not as a theory or definition, but as the pragmatists' attempt to say something interesting about the nature of truth and to suggest, in particular, that knowledge claims cannot be totally abstracted from contingent beliefs, interests, and projects. It is illicit to criticize the pragmatic "theory" of truth when pragmatists refuse to offer one. After all, the arguments of pragmatists and near pragmatists (e.g., Davidson, 1973; Rorty, 1982c; Wittgenstein, 1958) are *deconstructive*—an attempt to get philosophers to stop placing demands on concepts such as "truth," and "reality" that are impossible to meet, and generating insoluble pseudo problems in the process.

Pragmatism, Relativism, and Irrationalism

The alternative to the pragmatic perspective is the forced choice between truth as correspondence and truth as coherence. Correspondence theories identify truth with a relationship *between* language and reality; coherence theories identify truth with internal consistency among claims *within* a language. The problem with correspondence theories is ever knowing when the relationship between a language and reality holds. Because there is no way to prevent knowledge of the world from being in some sense conditioned by belief systems, there is no way to know when knowledge claims are pure. The problem with coherence theories is that they ignore the problem of the relationship between language and reality altogether. Because a theory can obviously be consistent but false (few theories have been abandoned because they were internally inconsistent), and because there can obviously be more than one internally consistent theory, knowledge becomes relative to belief systems (or conceptual schemes) and therefore irrational.

Pragmatists are often attributed with embracing a coherence theory, but this misrepresents their position. For pragmatists do not take sides on the problem of coherence versus correspondence theories of truth; instead, they reject the problem altogether. Davidson (1973), Rorty (1982c), and Putnam (1990) for instance, argue that for the problem to get off the ground, some Reality, some "given," totally independent of beliefs and knowledge claims, must exist; otherwise, there is no dilemma of either matching up language and reality or remaining trapped, so to speak, within one's own belief system. They deny that any sense can be made of a "given" that, by its very nature, can never be known, and therefore they deny that a dilemma exists about the nature of truth.

Pragmatists are also often attributed with embracing relativism and irrationalism. If embracing relativism means embracing the view that no fail-safe, eternal "neutral matrix" exists for determining what theories are correct, pragmatists are relativists; if embracing relativism means embracing the view that no grounds exist for rationally evaluating theories, they are not. Pragmatists supplant coherence and correspondence with criteria such as accuracy, scope, simplicity, consistency, and comprehensiveness (e.g., Kuhn, 1977; Quine, 1970) and contend that basing theory choice on these criteria entails not that science is irrational, but that scientific rationality simply does not fit the positivist conception. The pragmatic suggestion regarding research methodology is thus for researchers to forge ahead with "what works." Given a charitable interpretation of what pragmatists mean by this, and given the alternative of an invidious incompatibility thesis, the pragmatic alternative cannot be so easily dismissed[2].

Conclusion: Compatibilist Educational Research

The quantitative/qualitative distinction is applied variously to data, design and analysis, interpretation of results, and epistemological paradigms. At the level of data, educational researchers mix quantitative and qualitative data, both by employing variables on qualitative and quantitative scales and by quantifying qualitative (in the intentionalist sense) concepts. In this way, so-called quantitative studies are pregnant with qualitative concepts and inferences.

At the levels of design, analysis, and interpretation of results, quantitative and qualitative researchers differ chiefly in the assumptions they are willing to make and how much attention they pay to the "insider's perspective" and "experience-near" data. There are no doubt many important differences in the kinds of methods employed, but these differences are often blown out of proportion, to the point of positing two fundamentally divergent paradigms, two views of reality, and other such polar extremes. The existence of two sets of methods entails at most that having more than one set of tools is useful. In particular, the fact that quantitative analysis involves precise statistical inferences is analogous to the fact that one might be able to employ a deductive syllogism or two in a complex political argument. Numerous assumptions, hunches, conjectures, and value judgments loom large in designing and conducting research, and in evaluating proffered conclusions.

At the level of epistemological paradigms, philosophy of science has long since moved on, into a "new" or "post-positivist" era. Questions about methodology remain, but they ought not to be framed in way that presupposes the moribund positivist/interpretivist split. The fact that quantitative and qualitative methods indeed might be historical outgrowths of incompatible positivist and interpretivist epistemologies no more requires present-day researchers to endorse one or the other of these epistemologies than the fact that astronomy is an outgrowth of astrology requires present-day astronomers to square their predictions with their horoscopes.

To conclude in the spirit of pragmatism, the sort of methodological compatibilism I have been promoting has several practical consequences. Certain educational researchers will be made insecure by compatibilism insofar as it blurs methodological lines. That is, compatibilism does not permit researchers to isolate themselves within methodological paradigms that are impervious to the challenges and contributions of alternative perspectives. The criteria for evaluating educational research apply—or ought to apply—across research methods. Although few researchers can be expected to master and pursue both quantitative and qualitative methods, they need at least a rudimentary understanding of what alternative approaches can provide and, accordingly, they should bring a collaborative (rather than paradigm-clique) attitude to research.

For their part, certain philosophers will be made insecure by compatibilism insofar as it blurs the lines between epistemology and research practice. But in the end, a philosophical perspective is valuable just to the extent that it helps shape practice, and helping to shape a practice requires careful attention to just what the practice is.

Notes

1 Interestingly, Smith and Heshusius cite Rorty and Bernstein, apparently in support of the incompatibility thesis. This is more than a little puzzling, for Rorty and Bernstein have their feet squarely in compatibilism (pragmatism). Rorty (1982a) wants to "stop asking" and Bernstein (1983) wants to "move beyond" the very questions about realism versus idealism and objectivism versus relativism that Smith and Heshusius argue are at the bottom of the incompatibility thesis.

2 I make no pretense of having "defeated" realism and/or a correspondence theory of truth; my primary aim was to give pragmatism a fairer hearing than it typically receives.

Chapter 4

THE PERSISTENCE OF THE FACT/VALUE DOGMA: A CHARACTERIZATION AND CRITIQUE OF THE "RECEIVED VIEW"

Nearly twenty years after he wrote it, Michael Scriven's warning that the fact/value dogma "will continue to rise from the ashes" unless it is "rendered completely absurd by complete exposure" (1983, p. 81) retains considerable currency. Indeed, the fact/value dogma seems even more refractory than Scriven suggested. It has had no need to rise from the ashes because it has never been reduced to them. Although few social researchers nowadays would deny that social research is value-laden, their effort to reshape theory and practice to effectively deal with what this means has been timid, at best. This is reflected in the "received view" on the relationship between facts and values (House & Howe, 1999).

Although this view is by no means universal, it still represents mainstream thinking in social research. As a consequence, many social researchers who unflinchingly avow the idea that the social research is value-laden are as committed as ever to the fact/value dogma and to what it implies: that the subject matter to which social research applies its tools, as well as the findings it derives, can be and ought to be value-free.

In this chapter, I examine two illustrations of the received view. I begin with how it has been articulated and defended in the field of program evaluation, where it has received significant attention. I focus especially on the work of Campbell (1982) and Shadish et al. (1995). My aims here are to generally characterize this view and to expose its defects, reviewing and substantially extending the critique of the fact/value dogma initiated in Chapter 2. The received view in program evaluation can be straightforwardly extended to educational research. I make this connection explicit by examining the notion of "consequentialist validity" in educational testing (e.g., Messick, 1989; Shepard, 1993).

The Received View and Program Evaluation

I begin with an explication and critique of two major theses of the received view: (1) the radical undecidability thesis and (2) the emotive conception of democracy.

The Radical Undecidability Thesis

The radical undecidability thesis holds that pervasive disagreement is endemic to the domain of values and not subject to rational resolution. Associated with the thesis are ways to both account for and deal with such disagreement. Though distinguishable, these two aspects are not easy to disentangle.

Accounting for Undecidability

As indicated in Chapter 2, the pioneering evaluation theorist Donald Campbell provides one of the clearest and most concise accounts of the alleged undecidability of value claims. Here, again, is what he said:

> The tools of descriptive science and formal logic can help us implement values which we already accept or have chosen, but they are not constitutive of those values. Ultimate values are accepted but not justified. (1982, p. 123)

To review, Campbell perceives a sizeable epistemological gap between descriptive science, on the one hand, and values, on the other. Values are undecidable because they have no cognitive basis: they must be "chosen" and "accepted" but cannot be "justified." And if this sounds like noncognitivism in values—the positivist view—there is good reason. Campbell explicitly embraces the positivist's account of the fact/value distinction.

A contemporary version of Campbell's view is to be found in the influential *Foundations of Program Evaluation* (Shadish et al., 1995). Paralleling Campbell's descriptive science/values distinction, Shadish et al. distinguish "descriptive valuing" from "prescriptive valuing." In descriptive valuing, evaluators confine themselves to describing the values held by different stakeholders; in prescriptive valuing, evaluators incorporate and advance their own substantive value positions, for example, a particular conception of justice (e.g., House, 1980).

Like Campbell, Shadish et al. contend that evaluators should confine themselves to description, but their ostensive justification is somewhat different. Rather than giving an account along *epistemological lines* à la Campbell—that because values cannot be justified, evaluators cannot legitimately advance value judgments—they give an account more or less along *factual lines*—that because value disagreement is rife, it is not "practical" for evaluators to advance value judgements. I will say more about the criterion of practicality in the next section. First I suggest that Shadish et al. cannot successfully avoid presuming an epistemological gulf between factual (descriptive) claims and value (prescriptive) claims as the ultimate basis for their view, and I buttress the general critique of this presumption begun in Chapter 2.

Shadish et al. give repeated warnings against prescriptive valuing on the grounds that, unlike descriptive valuing, it is plagued with disagreement and undecidability. But the point here cannot be about avoiding disagreement and undecidability *per se*. Otherwise, the admonition would apply indifferently to all claims, including descriptive ones. That the admonition applies to a particular *kind* of disagreement and undecidability, namely, that attached to prescriptive claims, indicates that an alleged epistemological gulf between descriptive and prescriptive claims must underlie their call for evaluators to systematically identify and remove their own substantive value commitments. But the descriptive/prescriptive (fact/value) distinction is not straightforward and clean enough to do the work that Shadish et al. (and Campbell) require of it. To show why requires a bit of a digression.

There are at least two ways in which values might enter into scientific work, rendering it *value-laden*: by framing it and by describing its objects. I take it that there is little or no disagreement that values unavoidably frame scientific research, of all kinds. The dispute about framing is whether it is only *methodological* values that researchers *qua* researchers may embrace and promote, or whether they should (must) also embrace and promote *moral-political* values. This is a dispute I take up in the section on emotive democracy. Here I concentrate on the point that description frequently has an evaluative dimension, particularly in social research.

As I indicated in Chapter 2, the vocabulary of natural science has little or no need to incorporate an evaluative dimension into its concepts. Thus, concepts like "velocity" or "mass" in physics are value-free in all but the most restrictive uses of that term. To be sure, an indefinite number of isolated claims like "2+2=4," "the cat is on the mat," "Ms. Smith's third-grade class has 22 pupils," and so on, are also value-free. But it is a mistake to conclude from these examples that a sharp epistemological dividing line generally characterizes the relationship between description and evaluation. Where knowledge is squared with the kind of contemporary, holistic epistemology associated with notions such as "paradigms" and "conceptual schemes," context and background knowledge become all important in determining the meaning and implications of given claims, including their evaluative dimensions. This is especially so in social research.

Consider the following claim: "Class size has no discernible effect on achievement." "Achievement" is key here; it is of interest in educational research only because of its value-laden dimensions, i.e., its relationship to what we should pursue in education and how we should evaluate the success of educational policies and practices. This is perhaps most obvious when "achievement" is criticized for being too narrow a goal for education, as being culturally biased, and so forth, and this criticism is carried over to also apply to research on class size that uses achievement as it criterion. What can obscure the value-ladeness of research on class size—of educational research in general—is that value-ladeness is much less obvious when the meanings and implications of value-laden concepts such as achievement are not critically examined. But this doesn't mean educational research is ever value-free; it just means that underlying values are sometimes not in dispute, whether they should be or not.

To pursue the importance of underlying values a bit further, consider another claim: "Whites out score African Americans on the SAT." When isolated, this has the appearance of being value-free, of being a *brute fact*, if you will. But consider it against the background of the moral-political framework employed in the *Bell Curve* (Murray & Herrnstein, 1994). Within this framework, that Whites out score African Americans on the SAT warrants the inference that African Americans deserve their place in the social system. Now consider it against the background of the moral-political framework employed in *Savage Inequalities* (Kozol, 1991). Within this framework, the claim warrants the inference that African Americans wind up where they do in the social system because equal educational opportunity is denied to them. As these examples illustrate, certain claims are especially prone to serve as "inference tickets" (Toulmin, 1953) that permit one to move from one place to another in a conceptual scheme. Although the *brute fact* that Whites outscore African Americans on the SAT can be isolated, this is deceiving. It wouldn't hold any interest—be an *interesting* brute fact—if it didn't possess evaluative content and have a role to play in some value-laden framework. Compare "On average, Whites have more hairs on their heads than African Americans." Whether this is true or false holds little interest.

To amplify this point, compare the following:

- "Jones killed Smith with malice" and "Jones' actions led to Smith's death"

- "The project director stole 50K in project funds" and "The project director deposited 50K in project funds in his personal account"

- "Gay and lesbian youth suffer discrimination and oppression in public schools" and "Gay and lesbian youth are at risk in public schools"

In each of these pairs, the first description is more value-laden than the second. But these descriptions are not fundamentally different *qua* descriptions for that reason. Instead, they describe different states of affairs and, accordingly, have different truth conditions to satisfy. Changing their evaluative content merely serves to change what is being described. What is more, changing their evaluative content expressly to render them more value-neutral can compromise their ability to guide practice (Rorty, 1982b). In each of the above pairs, for example, the first description better targets problems and remedies—provides "inference tickets" to clearer destinations—than the second.

The presumption, then, of a sharp epistemological dividing line between description and evaluation (facts and values) that would permit social researchers to identify values and separate them from descriptions is untenable. A better way to characterize the relationship can be gleaned from the preceding discussion, namely, as a continuum of the degree to which description and evaluation overlap in the conduct of social research (House & Howe, 1999). Claims range from "Ms. Smith's third-grade class has 22 pupils," at the value-free end, to "Whites outscore African Americans on the SAT," in the middle, to "Gay and lesbian youth suffer discrimination and oppression in public schools," at the heavily value-laden end.

Dealing with Undecidability

The arguments of the preceding section significantly weaken the undecidability thesis by undermining the epistemological distinction it presupposes between description and evaluation. As I argued, Shadish et al. implicitly embrace just this distinction and are therefore vulnerable to the criticisms of it advanced in the previous section. Setting that issue aside, I now turn to their "practical" argument for the view that values should be rooted out, separated from facts, and set to one side in the conduct of evaluation research.

Time and again Shadish et al. criticize evaluation theorists for being impractical should they advocate substantive value commitments ("prescriptive valuing") on the part of evaluators. The basic contours of the argument (reconstructed so as to explicate tacit premises) are as follows: (1) the undecidability of value claims is a fact; (2) everyone knows this, including policymakers and stakeholders; (3) incorporating and advancing substantive values in the conduct, findings, and recommendations of an evaluation is prescriptive valuing; (4) given (1) and (2), policymakers and stakeholders will, as a rule, reject evaluations that involve prescriptive valuing on the part of evaluators; therefore, (5) evaluations that incorporate substantive values are, as a rule, impractical.

But impractical for what? Shadish et al. employ this argument as if what it means to be practical is always the same. But this is not so. The claim "X is practical (impractical)" is elliptical for "X is practical (impractical) as a means to Y." The "Y" they seem to consistently have in mind is successfully influencing policymaking. This is certainly an important goal of evaluation research. But is the evaluator who criticizes, say, the tobacco lobby's effort to escape regulation by the Federal Drug Administration necessarily a poor practitioner of her craft? What if her results and recommendations are ignored because she is accused of bias by the tobacco lobby for doing her own "prescriptive valuing" based on the adverse health effects of smoking? If successfully influencing policymaking is the only goal of evaluation, then evaluators would seem to be little more than consultants who provide the kinds of information those holding the reigns of power find useful.

Shadish et al. are not categorically opposed to prescriptive valuing on the part of evaluators. For example, they embrace ethical codes as a legitimate variety of prescriptive valuing. But here is the rub: *Once prescriptive valuing is acknowledged as legitimate, some argument is required to show why it should be so minimal.* The criterion of practicality is not up to the task, because some further criterion or criteria beyond having an influence on policymaking is required to fill out the formula "practical as a means to Y." As we shall see in the next section, Shadish et al. have a much broader (if unwitting) commitment to prescriptive valuing than they explicitly avow.

The Emotive Conception of Democracy

Shadish et al. often identify a "prescriptive theory" with a broad political theory, e.g., Rawls' (1971) theory of justice. They then invoke the undecidability thesis to attempt to show how employing prescriptive theories like Rawls' is to be avoided because it conflicts with fostering a "pluralism of values" (p. 456). They support this in two ways: (1) There are "credible alternatives," they say, to Rawls' theory (p. 456), Nozick's (1974) theory in particular. (2) "Justice," they say, "is just one moral concern in evaluation, along with human rights, equality, liberty, and utility" (p. 456). Shadish et al. conclude that because there is no way to decide between competing theories of justice or between justice and other values, evaluators should bracket all of this and confine themselves to "descriptive theory."

Their argument is far from convincing. First, they write as if they were providing an *alternative to employing a prescriptive theory*, when, in actuality, they are *employing an alternative prescriptive theory of their own*: Don't employ Rawls' and similar theories because that would violate fostering a pluralism of values. In this way, they are not the agnostics they claim to be, for they implicitly reject Rawls' theory. They implicitly reject Nozick's as well. The alternative prescriptive theory they implicitly embrace is "emotive democracy" (a name inspired by MacIntyre, 1981), which they use both to frame evaluation practice and to criticize other evaluation theorists who hold a different view.

Second, the fact that Rawls and Nozick disagree does not by itself imply that no one can be right about these matters. Despite rancorous disagreement, weren't the Emancipation Proclamation and the decision in *Brown v. the Board* right? And, to take this into the "descriptive" realm, because many initially disagreed with Galileo, does this imply that no one could be right about whether the earth revolves about the sun?

Every theory of evaluation presupposes some political theory (if only an informal one). There is simply no way to avoid this. The theory that Shadish et al. presuppose, "emotive democracy," is firmly rooted in the undecidability thesis: because values are immune from rationale examination, democracy is characterized as a scramble on the part of various interest groups to get their way, employing whatever methods and strategies prove effective. The substance of competing values is irrelevant, since a value is a value is a value. Consider the following concrete illustration, in which Shadish et al. criticize the idea that social programs should be evaluated in terms of how well they serve the needs of the disadvantaged:

> Many stakeholders in American social policy would dispute the assumptions and re-commendations of needs-based theories of justice about redressing social inequities ... the assumptions and recommendations of such egalitarian theories are probably not operational in U.S. social policy (Lindblom, 1977). When policy is being framed and implemented, participants in the policy process rarely seek to ensure that the needs of the most disadvantaged Americans are met before other needs ... recent history sug-gests that policy may be shaped as much or more by defense policy, health care costs, taxes, and priorities that serve constituencies other than the disadvantaged. Selecting criteria of merit from needs-based theories of justice may result in evaluations that differ dramatically from the terms used in policy debates. This can minimize the usefulness of such evaluations. (pp. 96-97)

The clear *prescriptive* message of this passage is that the disadvantaged can make no special claims relative to other interest groups, say, Fortune 500 CEO's, defense contractors, or wealthy investors who want a reduction in capital gains taxes. The claims of the disadvantaged ought to be treated as on a par with any others that may be thrown into the mix, and then only if they satisfy the "terms used in policy debates."

Shadish et al. may very well be accurate in their portrayal of how our political system in fact looks, functions, and the "terms of policy debates" it employs. But do they want to *prescribe* the status quo? Would they do the same in the antebellum South or pre- *Brown*? If so, they would still be committed to some kind of political framework that determines how society's goods ought be distributed, as well as who ought be heard and how.

Consistent with its emotive conception of democracy, the received view sanc-tions two roles for evaluation at its intersection with the political system and policymaking: *means depiction* and *interest group depiction*. Both are groun-ded in the undecidability thesis. They differ in the extremes to which they take these, however, as a consequence of how much (ungrounded) agreement they believe exists with respect to values.

Means Depiction

Means depiction is the role for evaluation that Donald Campbell's theory incorporates. The tacit assumption is that although values/ends evade "justi-fication" in a way the facts/means do not, there are nonetheless some ends that are (ought to be?) "accepted," for example, ameliorating poverty. The role for evaluation is to investigate the means by which such ends might be realized, and then to hand them over to policymakers for implementation. This role fits well with 60's-style liberalism, a time in which the effort to find the means to create the Great Society enjoyed widespread support.

Of course, 60's-style liberalism has since fallen on hard times, and the seeds of its demise were there all along. Because it incorporates the undecidability thesis, means depiction can foster progressive social change only so long as ends go largely unchallenged. When the agreement breaks down, as it did beginning in the mid 70's, no cognitive resources are available with which to argue that ends such as the elimination of poverty should be placed above ends such as boosting skier visits to Aspen.

A different slant on what is wrong with evaluation as means depiction is that it is much better suited to a technocratic society than to a democratic one (Fay, 1975; Howe, 1992). This criticism applies whether means depiction is working smoothly or not. Means, after all, are means only relative to some end. Adopting a given end, say, increased computer literacy, entails focusing evaluation on the limited array of means that may be used to accomplish this end. Consequently, such an investigation of means presupposes the value orientation of those who support this end from among many others that might compete for resources. This is anti-democratic insofar as ends (values) are presumed rather than negotiated. It results in the manipulation and control of the citizenry rather than in their participation.

Interest Group Depiction

Interest group depiction is associated with newer incarnations of the received view. The undecidability thesis remains in place. But gone is Campbell's faith in the power of social research to render credible judgments about means, and gone also is his assumption of a set of shared values that such means could serve to bring to fruition. In their place is a much more fragmented picture of means and ends. Rather than investigating grand means to grand ends, the role for evaluation is to depict the fragments by constructing "value summaries" for the plethora of stakeholders: "If X is important to you, then evaluand Y is good for the following reasons" (Shadish et al., 1995, p. 101). Evaluation confines itself to handing over a collection of such conditional statements to policymakers. This role fits well with 90's-style conservatism, a time in which skepticism of all kinds—about science, the professions, welfare state interventionism—is the rule of the day.

Interest group depiction is associated with an exceedingly feeble ideal of democracy in which very little, if anything, is done to redress imbalances in political power. It is patently obvious that disadvantaged groups are presently unable to have their interests equally represented in politics and policymaking. This requires no argument. Left to their own devices, there is no way the disadvantaged can have an equal voice. Thus, they are subject to having someone else's view of the good life imposed on them, rendering democracy a sham.

The obvious remedy is to have evaluators seek out and bring to the table the needs of the disadvantaged. But this remedy is explicitly blocked by Shadish et al. As we saw earlier, such a practice is to be avoided because it can "minimize the usefulness" of evaluations by couching them in a vocabulary not used in policy debates. Furthermore, and more far reaching in its implications, Shadish et al. insist that bringing the needs of the disadvantaged to the table violates the general prohibition against "prescriptive valuing" by presupposing a needs-based, egalitarian theory of justice. This is a principle that not only fails to foster democracy, it thwarts it by fortifying the power *status quo*.

Apparently, Shadish et al. would include the *interests* (versus *needs*) of the disadvantaged under the right conditions: if this (1) does not violate the vocabulary of policymaking and (2) the interests of the disadvantaged receive no special treatment, i.e., are treated as just one among other "value summaries" (e.g., "If you want to avoid going hungry, then oppose cuts in the food stamp program"). They also add this condition: (3) the disadvantaged should speak for themselves rather than have others speak for them; this is required to stay within the confines of descriptive valuing. I have already discussed the anti-democratic implications of the first two conditions. The third has such implications as well, and it also raises yet another problem for the attempt by Shadish et al. to distinguish descriptive from prescriptive valuing.

I derive the third condition from the way in which Shadish et al. take sides with Kenny against House's (1980) view that the interests of the disadvantaged should be represented in policymaking and should take priority over certain other interests (e.g., the Aspen ski industry's). Of course, Shadish et al. reject both of these features of House's theory, at least as general requirements. The bone of contention regarding condition (3) is House's additional claim that evaluators may (and sometimes should) speak for the interests of the disadvantaged. This is what Shadish et al. quote approvingly from Kenny:

> I am very suspicious of those who say they are speaking for the poor or disadvantaged when they themselves are not poor or disadvantaged. It strikes me that the highest form of elitism occurs when persons unchosen by the disadvantaged say that they speak for the disadvantaged or they say they take the disadvantaged's interests into account. Let us be concerned, but let us remember that we can only speak for ourselves. (in Shadish et al., 1995, p. 51)

Well, the disadvantaged didn't speak for themselves in the face of cuts in social welfare programs in the last quarter of the 20th century. Why not? Could it be that they (rightly) felt disenfranchised and hopeless? One doesn't have to be a paternalist to hold that the disadvantaged, through no fault of their own, are often not in a good position to speak for themselves—they can lack information and articulateness, time and transportation, political savvy about how things work, and can be mistrustful and intimidated.

True, there are real dangers in deciding what is best for groups from a distance (though attributing to everyone a desire for adequate food, shelter, health care, and education seems pretty safe). Thus, when evaluators clear the necessary hurdles placed in front of them by Shadish et al. regarding when it is legitimate to seek out and include the interests of the disadvantaged (conditions (1) and (2)), they are admonished to make sure the disadvantaged speak for themselves. Again, this is required in order for evaluators to stay within the confines of descriptive valuing: "Having the disadvantaged speak for themselves is descriptive valuing" (p. 51).

There must be some maneuver space in applying the requirement to have the disadvantaged speak for themselves. Unless evaluators are to be mere recorders of passing events, they must be permitted to provide relevant information, to prompt, probe, edit, translate, seek clarifications, recast, etc. It is difficult (impossible) to avoid these sorts of interactions in attempting to represent someone's views, even in their own voice. And here Shadish et al. seem to get tripped up by their descriptive/prescriptive dualism. For the implicit rationale for requiring the disadvantaged to speak for themselves is that who describes the perspective of the disadvantaged affects the prescriptive valuing that description contains. And what does this mean if not that descriptive valuing and prescriptive valuing cannot be systematically and comprehensively disentangled, if not that evaluators often can't do one without doing the other?

At the root of the difficulties for Shadish et al. is their view (or views) about the kind of things values are. Much of the time Shadish et al. seem to assume that values are like discrete, impenetrable pebbles. The evaluator's role is to gather these up and formulate "value summaries." Given this view, the descriptive valuing/prescriptive valuing distinction is assumed to be robust. As we have just seen, however, regarding the question of who should speak for the disadvantaged, Shadish et al. slide into another view, in which values are more like gelatin cubes, still discrete but easily reshaped by handling. Here the descriptive valuing/prescriptive valuing distinction is quite fragile. As it turns out, both of these views are dubious because they both assume that values are discrete and pre-existing, somehow out—or in—*there*, waiting to be described. There is an alternative.

By way of illustrating the alternative, suppose a social researcher were to ask me the following question:

> What do you think of changing the U.S. political system to a parliamentary one, on the model of Israel's?

I'd likely say something along the following lines:

> Well, I can see real advantages to a system in which minority views can be heard, even if they don't win out, in preference to our system in which all we hear are the views

of those who have captured a majority of votes by patching together watered-down, unimaginative, least controversial policies. But I really need more information. I'm not all that familiar with the Israeli system, and I assume that we would want to modify it to fit our situation as well.

Based on this exchange would it be right to say I "value" moving to the Israeli system? Probably not. But it would not be right to say I don't value it either. After further interaction, however, in which I could get my questions answered to my satisfaction, I might very well come down on one side or the other.

Many questions about who values what are like this, to one degree or another. That is to say, values are *emergent*. In the above example, suppose, after further interactions with the researcher in which the information I want is provided to me, I wind up supporting a move to a parliamentary system. Was this value there all along or was it newly constructed? It's hard to say. In one sense it was *there* all along, but could be uncovered only through dialogue and reflection. In another sense it was not *there* but constructed, for I couldn't articulate a position at the outset. But why worry about this question anyway? Shouldn't evaluators—social researchers in general—be concerned with what people believe upon reflection? Isn't this the most important and relevant sense of what they *really* believe *vis-à-vis* social policy initiatives? And, finally, isn't this what a genuine and robust democracy requires?

The Received View and Educational Testing

In the received view of program evaluation, evaluators must be on the alert to identify values and must isolate them from the means of promoting them revealed by social research. The very same approach predominates in research and policy analysis in the area of educational testing.

Educational measurement has been dominated historically by technicists. The general mode of operation is to abstract questions of test validity and bias from the values and the social conditions that surround test use. The problem of test validity is defined exclusively as one of obtaining accurate measurements. When the game is played by these rules, investigating the validity of testing is put squarely in the category of scientific investigation, and is thereby insulated from broader questions of values.

Recently, "consequentialists" have come to the fore in educational measurement (e.g., Messick, 1989; Shepard, 1993). Consequentialists deny the sharp distinction between scientific investigation and value judgments embraced by traditional technicists, and see questions of test validity and bias as unavoidably embedded in value-laden social aims and conditions. Accordingly, they hold that validity research requires explicating the values that underpin testing practices and investigating the intended and unintended social consequences of various uses to which tests are put.

What makes the idea of consequentialist validity germane to my purposes here is that it is generally taken to be a radical proposal *vis-à-vis* incorporating values into research on test validity. In my view, it is not radical at all. That it should be taken to be shows just how natural and seemingly unproblematic it has become to embrace the received view and proceed to separate values from the real scientific work of educational research.

Whatever one's position on educational testing, the elimination of bias is a minimal requirement of its just use. Questions of test bias are closely related to questions of test validity. Intuitively, a test (test use) is valid if it measures what it purports to and invalid if it does not. Bias is a kind of invalidity that arises relative to groups. In general, a test is biased against a particular group if it under-predicts their performance on the criterion of interest relative to some other group(s). For example, the SAT is charged with bias against women on the grounds that although women generally score lower than men, their scores correlate with higher college performance relative to men's.

The kind of bias just described is conventionally termed *predictive*. It is crucial to observe that establishing a strong relationship between test performance and performance on a criterion measure is insufficient to eliminate bias. In addition to the kind of predictive bias described so far, tests may also encounter the problem of criterion bias. First, the criterion measure with which a test is correlated may be a poor indicator of the performance ultimately of interest. For example, the SAT may be highly correlated with college GPA, but GPA, the criterion measure in this case, may be only weakly associated with college performance in its fuller sense. I call this *criterion measure bias* (which is simply a variant of predictive bias). Second, the criterion of performance itself may be biased, independent of how strongly it is associated with a criterion measure and how well the criterion measure correlates with test scores. I call this *essential* criterion bias.

Essential criterion bias (henceforth, simply criterion bias unless otherwise indicated) may take two forms: across and within. Across-criterion bias occurs when test performance is too heavily emphasized relative to other qualifications. Over-reliance on testing inflates the importance of criteria that it can accurately measure—various academic talents and accomplishments, in particular—to the point of viewing these criteria as all-purpose qualifications that should be negotiable currency in virtually any arena.

Within-criterion bias is bias in its most insidious form. Criterion measures may be perfectly matched to the demands of a given domain of performance, including being appropriately weighted, but nonetheless give rise to advantages and disadvantages associated with characteristics such as race, social class, and gender. For example, if the curricula and pedagogy of the U.S. educational system are as heavily biased in favor of white males as they are so frequently charged of being, then criteria of performance are *ipso facto* biased in favor of white males as well. Under these kinds of conditions, eliminating predictive bias from educational tests can do little to eliminate bias in its fuller, *essential* sense. All it can do is improve predictions of who will do well in terms of the criteria of performance associated with those who have historically enjoyed advantages within biased institutional arrangements.

Within-criterion bias, then, is one way of explaining (as well as justifying) the claims by various marginalized and oppressed groups—women, African Americans, Native Americans, Latinos, and others—that testing practices are biased against them. The frequent rejoinder by measurement experts that such charges of bias are often unwarranted is correct only insofar as "bias" is employed in its technical, predictive sense, in which the sole question is how well predictor and criterion measures correlate.

In the absence of a common understanding of what counts as bias, controversies about whether tests are biased are often at cross-purposes (e.g., Madaus, 1994). In ordinary language, one would infer that the use of an unbiased test for selection is *prima facie* fair. But where "unbiased" is confined to its technical meaning, this inference is not warranted— the "inference ticket" is counterfeit. For a test use that is unbiased in the technical, predictive sense may be infected with essential criterion bias (across as well as within). The danger here, potential as well as real, is that claims that test uses are valid and unbiased, while made on the basis of technical meanings, will trade on ordinary meanings to defend testing practices: "The use of test X is *fair* (in the ordinary sense) because it is not *biased* (in the technical sense)."

The so-called "consequentialist" conception in educational measurement is motivated by the aim of more thoroughly integrating values into the concept of test validity. Shepard (1993) suggestively likens the difference between the traditional technicist conception of validity and her consequentialist conception to the difference between settling for "truth in labeling" and demanding that testing also be "safe and effective." But she fails to make her case. She fails, that is, to distance herself very far from the technicist conception of validity and the received view that goes with it.

Shepard's commitment to separating the "science" of validity research from values is explicit in her discussion of the use of a multiple criteria approach for admission to selective colleges. She defends the use of the SAT as an adjunct to other criteria, such as music or athletic talent, minority group status, and geographical distribution. (Here she is concerned with what I referred to earlier as across-criteria bias.) Contrasting scientific questions with value choices, she claims:

> At one level, examination of these selection practices might provoke a debate between different philosophical positions. Should decisions be guided by meritocratic or other theories of social justice .... At a more technical level, [multiple criteria] can be defended "scientifically" given that academic predictors are both incomplete and fallible

predictors of success .... Therefore, [the] value perspective [associated with multiple criteria] holds that colleges can reasonably select among qualified applicants using criteria aimed at other goals such as increasing the diversity of perspectives represented among their students. This value choice cannot be resolved within the validity framework but should be made explicit and examined for consequences as part of the validity investigation .... (1993, p. 435)

This passage is relevant to both forms of criterion bias, and it may be used to illustrate the inability of Shepard's consequentialist framework to address either. Regarding across-criteria bias, Shepard holds that criteria other than test scores may be "reasonably" employed. However, in the absence of some more substantive value commitment (e.g., an egalitarian theory of justice), there is no way to determine whether, more than just being "reasonable," the criterion of race indeed ought to be included in selection decisions. Regarding within-criterion bias, in the absence of some more substantive value commitment (e.g., to a culturally responsive curriculum) there is no way to determine whether the criteria of success are indeed (essentially) biased against certain groups. To make matters worse, where (essential) within-criterion bias is present, the SAT would be objectionable as a selection device even if it were an infallible and complete predictor of "success"!

The consequentialist view is thus simply a more sophisticated version of the traditional technicist view. Although the issue of what constitutes an acceptable "scientific" evaluation is clearly more complex on the consequentialist view, it is nonetheless conceived in a way that conditions the scientific question of what uses of testing are valid on "value choices" that are beyond the purview of validity research. Thus, the claim that "X use of testing is valid" is always a disguised hypothetical—always of the form "X use of testing is valid, *if* you want to promote Y" (where Y is some value commitment, ranging from relatively specific practices like talent tracking to general theories of justice). Suppose that the Y in question is maximizing economic efficiency and a test X has been devised that stratifies school children into tracks in a way that achieves Y. The consequentialist, it would seem, can have no objection either to the claim that X is valid or to implementing X, because she can have no objection to Y. In this way, the consequentialist conception retains the same fundamental bifurcation between validity research and value judgments as the technicist conception. It retains the "truth in labeling" criterion as well.

What has been greeted by many as a radical move to breach the science/values divide in validity research winds up being nothing but a dyed-in-the-wool example of the received view. To be sure, the place of values isn't theorized to the same extent in the arena of validity research as it is in program evaluation. For the kind of explicit statements by evaluation theorists like Campbell—to maintain "a vigorously exhorted fact value-distinction,"—and Shadish, et al.— to avoid "prescriptive valuing"—are missing. Nonetheless, a rigid fact/value distinction is there, taken for granted in the explication of how scientific and value judgments are related.

Conclusion: Why the Fact/Value Dogma Persists

Why, despite the nearly unanimous repudiation of positivism and, with it, the admonition to keep social research value-free, does the received view retain such widespread acceptance? There are at least three reasons.

First, the putative epistemological gulf between facts and values is often illustrated by juxtaposing claims such as "Grass is green" with claims such as "Abortion is morally wrong." Wittgenstein says somewhere that we are often led astray by an "unbalanced diet of examples." This is one of those cases.

These examples pick out an uncontroversial factual claim and compare it to a controversial value claim. To turn the table, compare "Light is composed of waves" with "Torturing children for fun is good." Choosing "Abortion is wrong" to establish the undecidability thesis masks the underlying agreement on values that characterizes social life and that makes it possible. In addition to "don't torture children for fun," consider: "don't gratuitously spit on or punch a passerby;" "don't covet your neighbor's possessions;" "don't burn down your neighbor's house;" "don't falsify data." Alternatively, choosing "Grass is green" to illustrate the decidability of factual claims masks the disagreement that so often characterizes the cutting edge of science. In addition to the wave theory of light, consider the heliocentric theory of the solar system (in Galileo's time); the collision theory of the disappearance of the dinosaurs (which seems to have won out); the big bang; and so on.

Contributing to the unbalanced diet of examples so as to further encourage the perception of a vast epistemological divide between science and the moral-political domain is the failure to recognize that scientific communities are relatively small and insulated, incorporate a relatively restricted range of interests, and engage in disagreements that remain largely hidden from public view. By comparison, the moral-political community is huge, the interests it incorporates are vast, and the disagreements within it are open for everyone to see.

Second, that normative principles are as much a part of the "tools of descriptive science and logic" (Campbell, 1982) as they are of moral-political discourse often goes unnoticed. Such principles amount to "prescriptive valuing" in each case, for each specifies good reasoning in terms of regulative values. Compare "Violating the law of non-contradiction is irrational" and "Deliberately falsifying data is wrong." Rationality and science, no less than morality and politics, are regulated by substantive cognitive values.

Finally, the ocular model—construing knowledge as a "mirror of nature" (Rorty, 1979)—no doubt figures in to the received view in a fundamental way. One can check, by looking, to see whether grass is green. On the other hand, however unimpeachable the prohibition against torturing children for fun may be, there is no way to check it to see if it mirrors the way things are, out there, in reality.

There is a difference here, but why not accept it as just that? Why not conclude that it marks a difference *within* the domain of knowledge rather than *between* knowledge and some pretender? For example, our explanation of persons that persistently claim to see pink elephants is that they are irrational, mentally defective, out of touch. The same serves as our explanation of persons who insist it's okay to torture children for fun. In this way, the two cases are epistemologically quite similar (see, e.g., Taylor, 1995a).

I am not suggesting that no differences exist between factual and value claims, between science and politics, between "descriptive valuing" and "prescriptive valuing." I am suggesting that the gap between them is much narrower than proponents of the received view believe. I am also suggesting that there is much cognitive work to be done in the arena of "prescriptive theory"—work that advocates of the received view have largely sought to avoid.

Could it be that social researchers who embrace the received view don't really intend to, or believe they can, check their moral-political commitments at the door to social research. Perhaps what they have in mind is a moral-political strategy: "Okay, you say testing for track placement accomplishes consequences C. *Let's bracket the question of whether the stratified system presupposed by talent tracking programs is morally defensible. I don't want to get into that argument now.* Let's just see whether C really happens."

In the rough and tumble of educational of policy-making the italicized portion of the above remark is likely to go unstated. But this is different than saying it's not there, or, *à la* Shadish et al., it shouldn't be there. Too often, *strategic* reasons for keeping quiet on moral matters—I'll only get myself into hot water; I'll make matters worse; I can't win this one in the present political climate—are identified with *epistemological* reasons for keeping quiet—"purely value choices" are separable from and beyond the purview of scientific research; I am bound by my role as a scientist to keep quiet on such matters. There is a significant danger in conflating the epistemological and strategic reasons for muting value claims: social researchers who fail to see the difference end up believing they can (and should) cull out moral-political matters and set them to one side as they go about the business of pure science. But they cannot do this. Thinking they can only insulates value commitments from critical examination and thereby serves the power *status quo*. If values are not subject to "scientific" (read: systematic and rational) examination, political power and influence is all there is to fall back on.

II

INTERPRETIVISM AND THE NEW DIVIDES

Chapter 5

THE INTERPRETIVE TURN

Rabinow and Sullivan (1979) coined the phrase the "interpretive turn" to describe the epistemological shift underway in the social sciences in the mid to late 20th century, away from positivism and toward interpretivism. That Rabinow is an anthropologist and Sullivan is a philosopher symbolizes the merging of the social sciences and the humanities associated with this development. Charles Taylor addresses the point explicitly in his seminal "Interpretation and the Sciences of Man" (1987), where he rejects the view that there can be any scientifically neutral, impersonal language (a central tenet of positivism) with which to describe and interpret human activities. Rather, he says, "we have to think of man (sic) as a *self-interpreting* animal . . . there is no such thing as the structure of meanings for him independently of his interpretation of them . . . " (p. 46, emphasis added). This general perspective provides the epistemological underpinning for the current emphases in the social sciences and humanities on the cultural embededness of human identities and interests, and on including hitherto marginalized or excluded "voices" in our various conversations.

If the interpretive turn has not completely won out in educational theory, it is certainly in ascendancy. And this development has prompted new divides that are highly germane to educational research but that also has far reaching consequences for curriculum, pedagogy, and the political mission of education. In this chapter I portray and evaluate these divides in terms of three broad issues: epistemology, politics, and the ontology of the self. In each case I compare two versions of interpretivism: what I call the *postmodernist* and the *transformationist* perspectives (to be elaborated below).

Developing this analysis will require negotiating some pretty treacherous conceptual ground. For one of the things that characterizes the new divides is that the terms in which they are couched—interpretivism, postmodernism, constructivism, deconstructionism, and so forth—are not only employed in different ways by different people. The terms are also sometimes quite explicitly contested. There is no way I can sort through all of the conceptual ambiguity and controversy the new divides engender in this chapter. So I'll do the next best thing: acknowledge the difficulty and specify the meanings I attach to central terms. I'll provide some clarifications here at the outset and some others as my analysis unfolds.

By "interpretivism" I mean the broad epistemological view described above, not a particular research method or set of research methods. Although interpretivism is more closely linked (both historically and conceptually) with qualitative than quantitative methods, the general interpretivist perspective need not jettison quantitative methods. The idea that social and educational researchers are precluded from employing both qualitative and quantitative methods is a thesis of the "old" quantitative/qualitative divide that I argued in Chapter 3 should be put behind us.

By "postmodernism" I mean a certain perspective on the interpretive turn: that the Enlightenment political philosophy and epistemology dominant over approximately the last three and a half centuries are at a dead end, that modernity has "exhausted itself" (Lyon, 1994). The task of social research and philosophy is to "deconstruct," "denormalize," and "dismantle" modernity's still quite powerful presence.

By "transformationism" I mean another perspective on the interpretive turn: that although significantly flawed, much of the emancipatory project of modernity can be and ought to be preserved. The task of social research and philosophy is to see this project through.

As I said above, my analysis requires negotiating some treacherous conceptual ground, and the postmodernist/transformationist distinction presents some special problems in this vein. Significant differences exist on the question of who qualifies as a postmodernist. Derrida, Foucault, and Lyotard are on most lists; Rorty and Wittgenstein are on some (e.g., Beck, 1994); and one even includes Dewey (e.g., Doll, 1993). To make matters worse, some of those who often turn up on these lists explicitly disclaim the description (Foucault is a prime example of this) and others who turn up, are more often seen as alternatives to the postmodernist stance (Dewey is a prime example of this). Still, I can find no better term than "postmodernism" to represent one side of the new divides. The term is ubiquitous, many thinkers embrace it, and many others line up against it (or what they think it is).

"Transformationist" presents similar problems. It collapses into one category critical theorists (e.g., Jurgen Habermas), pragmatists (e.g., John Dewey), and certain feminists (e.g., Nancy Frazer). Frazer (1995) suggests the term "neopragmatism," which pretty well captures what I have in mind by transformationism. But I want to avoid introducing the additional controversy associated with employing this term. Despite their differences, which can be vast, the thinkers

I call "transformationists" are united in their opposition to postmodernism, or at least to a "strong" (Benhabib, 1995) version of it that they accuse of being radically relativistic, hyperskeptical, and nihilistic.

The postmodernist versus transformation framework has the virtue of setting the new divides into sharp relief, and capturing several general themes that are currently animating important controversies within educational theory and practice. On the other hand, I will suggest toward the end of this chapter that, in education at least, postmodernists and transformationists are not (or need not be) be at loggerheads, that each is committed both to criticizing and dismantling ("deconstructing") and transforming unjust and undemocratic educational practices.

Epistemology

Interpretivists share a constructivist epistemology, broadly construed. "Constructivists" in this sense may be set over and against classical empiricists and their offspring, the positivists. Interpretivists reject what Dewey called the "spectator view" of knowledge—the view that knowledge is built up piece by piece, by accumulation of an ever growing and increasingly complex arrangement of passively received, *neutral* observations. Instead, knowledge is *constructed* in the sense that it is a product of human interests, purposes and prior conceptions. On this view, the findings of social research are culturally and historically contingent, as well as laden with moral and political values.

Interpretivists face a formidable problem. On their account, is knowledge *merely* a cultural-historical artifact? Is it *merely* a collection of moral and political values? Does it *merely* serve certain interests and purposes? Postmodernists and transformationists offer different answers to these questions. Postmodernists seem to answer "yes" to these questions—or at least seem to have no grounds for answering "no." Consider Lyotard's definition of postmodernism: "I define *postmodern* as incredulity toward metanarratives" (1987, p.74). Briefly, a meta-narrative is a grand legitimating story, one important feature of which is its abstraction from time, place, and culture. Meta-narratives include grand epistemological stories such as the inevitable progress of science, and grand political stories such as Marxism and liberalism.

The Marxist and liberal traditions each embrace the goal of the emancipation of humankind, and postmodernists are highly suspicious of them for precisely this reason. Because the goal of emancipation incorporates a peculiarly Western epistemology, pursuing it serves, as Lyotard says, to "terrorize" peoples who had no part in writing it. It is, after all, a time-, place-, and culture-bound story of human knowledge and, accordingly, is a very bad fit for many socio-cultural groups. Worse, by presupposing certain conceptions of knowledge and rationality, it masks the manner in which modern Western societies oppress the many Others that exist within them and is thus a bad story for Western societies themselves. In the end, it blunts rather than fosters emancipation (e.g., Ellsworth, 1992).

Michel Foucault (1987) shares Lyotard's attitude toward meta-narratives and would supplant them with what he calls "genealogy." Foucault's method is to unearth (he has also employed the related notion of archeology) the historical antecedents that have given rise to the rationalization of modern institutions. For Foucault, rationality is irremediably historical and contingent, and there can be no extra-historical touchstones—meta-narratives—of the kind philosophers have sought since Plato. Related to this, knowledge and power are inextricably wedded in "regimes of truth" that function to "normalize" persons, that is, to render them acquiescent and "useful" *vis-à-vis* the institutions of modern society.

This description of the postmodernist incredulity toward meta-narratives should be sufficient to elucidate the basis for the general criticism that so routinely leaps to the minds of critics: that postmodernism is hopelessly relativistic and self-defeating, that it cannot, if consistently held, justify any knowledge claims whatsoever. For if all knowledge claims are thoroughly context-bound and are *merely* masks for interests and power, are not any that postmodernists might advance themselves also possessed of these features? Is not knowledge, then, just an illusion? And are not radical relativism, nihilism, and moral-political paralysis the unavoidable implications?

To be sure, postmodernists do not embrace these implications. Foucault (1987) seeks through his forms of analysis to displace seeming self-evidentness about normalcy and the practices that go with it, and he has a definite, albeit open-ended, political project here. Lyotard (1987) embraces the concept of justice but would replace the modernist conception that relies on consensus ("homology") with a postmodernist conception that facilitates the expression of difference ("parology").

Transformationists believe these kinds of moves simply won't work. Because of postmodernism's "hyper-skepticism" (Barber, 1992), postmodernists either have no way of getting their project off the ground in the first place, or leave what constitutes defensible political practice so uncharted as to have no destination.

Transformationists join postmodernists in rejecting the traditional philosophical quest for ultimate epistemological touchstones that transcend contingent human experience. But "overcoming epistemology," to use Charles Taylor's phrase (1995b), does not entail what they see the postmodernists doing: abandoning knowledge and rationality as illusory. Transformationists see their task as working out defensible conceptions of knowledge and rationality that have contingent human experience as their basis. In this way, the transformationist project is continuous with the emancipatory project of the Enlightenment. The postmodernist project, by contrast, is discontinuous. It seeks a fundamental break—or "rupture."

As I said before, among transformationists may be counted pragmatists, critical theorists, and (certain) feminists.[1] Thomas Kuhn (1962, 1977) perhaps provides the best general description of the transformationist epistemological view when he likens it to Darwinian evolution. In short, there exists no acontextualized criterion of knowledge toward which science must move. Instead, scientific theories are supported to the extent that they better handle the problematic than their competitors. A sort of bootstrapping characterizes scientific knowledge. Criteria for making these judgments exist, but they may not be mechanically applied, have no ultimate foundation, and are not settled once and for all.

Kuhn's emphasis, of course, is scientific paradigms, and the contours of his thesis are widely known, if not also widely accepted. More germane to my purposes here is the less familiar and less discussed (in the education literature at least) issue of moral epistemology.

Michael Walzer distinguishes two ways of doing moral philosophy:

> One way to begin the philosophical enterprise is to walk out of the cave, leave the city, climb the mountain, fashion for oneself . . . an objective and universal standpoint . . . . But I mean to stay in the cave, in the city, on the ground. Another way of doing philosophy is to interpret to one's fellow citizens the world of meanings we share. Justice and equality can conceivably be worked out as philosophical artifacts, but a just or an egalitarian society cannot. If such a society isn't already there— hidden, as it were, in our concepts and categories—we will never know it correctly or realize it in fact. (1983, p. xiv)

Charles Taylor (1995a) employs a distinction similar to Walzer's by identifying two models of practical reason: "apodictic" and "ad hominem." The apodictic model requires that there be (1) some independent criterion, uncontaminated by any particular system of beliefs, values, and dispositions, against which to check the claims of practical reason and (2) some failsafe procedure by which to determine whether the criterion is met. But this sets an impossible standard, one that even natural science can't meet. In terms of this standard, practical reasoning—the reasoning that applies in morals and politics—collapses into subjectivism, relativism, and nihilism, and the accompanying belief that moral and political claims are based on mere prejudice or bias.

But this follows only if there is no alternative way to construe practical reason, and Taylor believes there is: the ad hominem model. Taylor begins with a fact about practical reason that I, too, have noticed. Moral claims are often much more complex than they first appear. They almost always may be qualified when challenged with some form of "special pleading" that excuses or redefines what is being advocated. Consider the charge that the high stakes testing movement shows a callused disregard for diversity and threatens to further disadvantage groups that have historically fared poorly in schools. Now consider the "special pleading" exemplified in proponents of these kinds of policies: "No, you are wrong, we really want to *help* the disadvantaged. Rigor and accountability are the best way to do this." Even outrageous moral claims exhibit this pattern, as Taylor observes in the case of the practical reasoning of Nazis.

> [Nazis] never attack the ban on murder of conspecifics frontally. They are always full of special pleading: for instance, that their targets are not of the same species, or that they have committed truly terrible crimes which call for retaliation, or that they present a mortal danger to others. (1995a, p. 35)

Taylor uses the "special pleading" phenomenon and the underlying agreement it implies as the basis for the following picture of practical reason:

> The task of [practical] reasoning, then, is not to disprove some radically opposed first premise (say killing people is no problem), but rather to show how the policy is unconscionable on premises which both sides accept, and cannot but accept . . . its job is to show up special pleas. On this model . . . practical argument starts off on the basis that my opponent shares at least some of the fundamental dispositions toward good and right which guide me. The error comes from confusion, unclarity, or unwillingness to face some of what he (sic) can't lucidly repudiate; and reasoning aims to show up this error. (1995a, p.36)

In the case of the high stakes testing movement, the job of reason is to show how its associated policies can only further damage the prospects of the disadvantaged; in the case of the Nazis, it is to show that their theories of racial superiority and perception of the Jewish threat are preposterous. (This is reason's "job;" whether it will win the day in either of these cases is another question.)

This conception of practical reason dovetails with the broader interpretivist epistemology of social research. Interpretivists hold, contra positivism, that just as social science is irremediably theory-laden, it is irremediably value-laden as well (and see Chapters 2 and 4). Social scientific reasoning is value-laden-*cum*-interpretive-*cum*-constructivist and is thus shot through and through with practical reasoning.

Transformationists argue that postmodernism's indiscriminate attack on reason winds up nullifying *all* knowledge claims, including any advanced by postmodernists themselves. As Benjamin Barber (1992) puts it:

> Reason can be a smoke screen for interest, but the argument that it is a smoke screen itself depends on reason—or we are caught up in an endless regression in which each argument exposing the dependency of someone else's argument on arbitrariness and self-interest is in turn shown to be self-interested and arbitrary. (p. 109)

It is beyond the scope is this chapter to more fully develop this line of argument. (I take up similar issues in Chapters 7 and 8.) Generally speaking, ad hominem challenges such as the one exemplified by Barber are frequently employed against postmodernists to show that they cannot consistently disavow reason. This is an especially damaging form of criticism when applied to educational theorists who would claim allegiance to postmodernism. Why this is so will become clear as my arguments further unfold.

The Ontology of the Self

Ontology is that part of philosophy that concerns itself with the kinds of entities that exist and the features they possess. For example, do numbers exist? In what sense? Where can we find them? How about social structures? Do selves exist? What features, if any, do different selves share? How are selves formed? Are selves relatively stable or always in flux?

In the previous section, I described interpretivists as embracing a constructivist conception of knowledge (a claim which will be fleshed out in greater detail in Chapter 6). This feature of interpretivism renders the philosophical distinction between epistemology and ontology considerably more artificial than my way of dividing up this chapter may suggest (and see Taylor, 1987). For how human beings know and are known, and what knowledge consists of, is inextricably bound up with the kinds of things human beings are. And there is a further complication. Because human beings actively construct their social reality, the kinds of things human beings are is not necessarily the kinds of things they *must* or *ought to be*. Thus, given the value-ladeness of the description of human behavior discussed in Chapter 4, distinguishing the moral-political from the ontological is also artificial.

Be they postmodernists or transformationists, interpretivists are like-minded in their rejection of the positivist-inspired behaviorist conception of human nature, in which human beings are portrayed as passive recipients of stimuli, explicable in terms of conditioning by exogenous causes. Interpretivists hold that human beings are self-creating, or, as Brian Fay (1987) puts it, "activist" in their behavior. That is to say, it is not as if human beings are simply pushed to and fro by existing social arrangements and cultural norms. Instead, they actively shape and reshape these constraints on behavior. But there is a problem, and it parallels the one discussed earlier in connection with the nature of knowledge. Are human beings *completely* active? Is positivist-behaviorist characterization of them *totally* erroneous?

Insofar as postmodernists seek to "deconstruct" the workings of social structures and transformationists seek to "undistort" communication, each presupposes that human beings are not altogether active, that they can be unwittingly pushed to and fro by unseen and unknown causes. Beyond here postmodernists and transformationists diverge.

Postmodernists ascribe to the traditional liberal and Marxist "metanarratives" a commitment to an essential human self, a fixed model of human nature, to which all humankind should aspire and in terms of which all should be measured—things like "rational autonomy" and "species being," respectively. Postmodernists emphasize that, contrary to these "essentialist" conceptions, identities come in many forms, associated with race, class, and gender, among others. Identities must be seen as neither unified nor fixed, but as various and continually "displaced/replaced" (e.g., Lather, 1991a). "De-centering" is the watchword: placing the universal Everyman allegedly presupposed by Marxist and liberal meta-narratives at the center can only function to "normalize" and "terrorize" the many Others on the margins.

On the transformationist view (and here I use John Searle, 1995, as my example[2]), maintaining that something is real does not entail maintaining that it cannot be "constructed," much less that it must be essential and unchangeable. Automobiles, for example, would not be real if this were generally true. But consider money, the existence and nature of which is much less a "brute fact" than automobiles. Money is what Searle calls an "institutional fact"—a kind of fact that grows out of and would not exist but for human social arrangements and "collective intentionality." Nonetheless, money does not come into or go out of existence on the basis of what *individual* people believe or "construct." For example, suppose someone owes me $1,000. I cannot reject cash payment and demand gold because I happen to believe that currency is worth no more than the paper it is printed on. Whether I like it or not, currency is legal tender for the payment of debts.

The situation is parallel in the case of Searle's less formal, "social facts." Take gender. To be sure, there have been and continue to be institutional facts associated with the feminine gender (e.g., exclusion from voting in the past and exclusion from certain forms of military duty today). But more far-reaching are shared beliefs, expectations, know-hows, and practices that make up the social facts of gender. In Western societies, the feminine gender historically has been identified with nurturing and preserving relationship, on the one hand, and with a lack of the capacity for abstract reasoning, on the other. Women thus have been historically directed into activities such as homemaking, nursing, and elementary school teaching and away from engineering, politics, and science. Independent of what individual girls and women believe—and like it or not— there is a "'gender regimen" (Connell, 1987) associated with a particular kind of feminine identity that is, in turn, associated with a large complex of social facts that shape it.

These social facts must be reckoned with in thinking about identity. Changing our being requires a good deal of time and effort, and there is no guarantee of success. Partly because of this people often do not want to change and believe it is oppressive to expect them to. Instead, people want "recognition" of who they are (Taylor, 1994). And if this general observation about the phenomenology of the self were not true, it would be very difficult to make any sense whatsoever out of the demands to recognize diversity so prominent on the current political and educational scenes.

As the preceding paragraph suggests, there is no way to completely separate moral-political commitments from a conception of human nature. This echoes for a second time my remarks at the beginning of this section, and I will develop the implications in greater detail later. Here I will temporarily ignore the moral-political dimensions in order to look still further into the controversy between postmodernists and transformationists about the ontology of the self.

Searle (1995) employs the concept of "background of intentionality" to describe the peculiar context of human behavior and development. Against both mentalism (all human behavior is explicable in terms of conscious or unconscious understanding and intent) and behaviorism (all human behavior is explicable in terms of physical movements), Searle maintains that human beings possess the natural capacity to gain the know-hows required to respond to shared social and institutional facts in accordance with normative expectations, largely in virtue of their natural capacity to use language. Within this general framework, Searle develops the following general schema to explicate the ontological status of social facts: "X counts as Y in Z." To again take Searle's favorite example, money, the U.S. dollar bill (X) counts as legal tender (Y) in the U.S. (Z). One of Searle's fundamental points is that unlike gold, for example, there is nothing about the physical features of a paper currency that gives rise to its value and the normatively sanctioned behaviors that surround it. Rather, its value, its counting as legal tender, is a result of "collective intentionality."

Gender, race, and a whole host of other social categories can be viewed on a similar model, though it might be more suggestively formulated as X *marks* Y in Z. Race and gender (X's) each serve to mark a constellation of normatively sanctioned behaviors (Y's) associated with various contexts (Z's), including the context of schools. (Here I remind the reader that I am ignoring the issue of whether the norms in question are good. Norms need not be morally justifiable to regulate human behavior.) In this way, although social categories (X's) have no essence independent of what humans have constructed, they, like money, are no less real for that.

Gaining the know-hows associated with collective intentionality and learning how to negotiate the social terrain is a long and complex task. And because identity formation is "dialogical," as Charles Taylor says (1994), individuals unavoidably incorporate into their identities the normative structure associated with social categories and practices. Through many different dialogues in many different contexts people learn what it is to be a man, a woman, to be gay or lesbian, or to be an African American high school student.

Postmodernists who suggest that identities are constantly "displaced/replaced" (e.g., Lather, 1991a) must concede that selves have to remain in place at least long enough to be the object of deconstruction. In the case of women, for instance, they may sometimes celebrate the traditional feminine identity they have formed, as in "gynocentric" feminism (Young, 1990a), and may sometimes lament it, as in feeling like "a fraud" (Ornstein, 1995). Some similar form of ambivalence—coming out versus remaining closeted, being oppositional versus "acting white," for example—is characteristic of all marginalized groups. And this phenomenon, like the demand for recognition, makes sense only if human identities are relatively stable.

It should be observed that the general characterization of the ontology of the self provided by thinkers like Searle and Taylor is not one with which post-modernists necessarily disagree. The general idea that identity formation is "dialogical" is not one that postmodernists would find problematic. Further-more, identity can be stable and, indeed, real. As Foucault (1979) says,

> It would be wrong to say the soul is an illusion, or an ideological effect. On the contrary, it exists, it has reality, it is produced permanently, around, on, within the body by the functioning of a power that is exercised . . . on those one supervises, trains and corrects, over madmen, children at home and in school . . . This is the historical reality of [the] soul, which, unlike the soul represented by Christian theology, is not born in sin and subject to punishment, but is born rather out of methods of punishment, supervision and constraint. (p. 29)

This leaves the controversy about the self between postmodernists and trans-formationists quite unsettled. Both are "constructivists" with respect to the ontology of the self: they agree that it is formed through social interaction and that it has no transcendent essence. Then how do postmodernists and trans-formationists differ with respect to the self? The passage from Foucault points in the direction of an answer. For him (and postmodernists in general, I think) one must be ever wary of the "normalizing" and sinister influences that social forces have on the formation of selves, and be constantly at the ready to ex-pose, "deconstruct," and throw them off. For tranformationists, "normalizing" processes may be good. Education is—or ought to be—such a process.

The ontology of the self cannot be viewed in the abstract. As I observed several times before, it is thoroughly entangled with epistemology. As the last several paragraphs show, it is also thoroughly entangled with what (if anything) is adopted as the moral-political mission of education. And it is here where the differences between postmodernists and transformationists are perhaps most perspicuous.

Politics

Neither transformationists nor postmodernists believe present social arrange-ments are just and democratic, and both seek to identify social structures and norms that serve to oppress people. Each, then, embraces "deconstruction" in this sense. What divides them is the reason for engaging in deconstruction and what should follow in its wake.

In the extreme, the activity of deconstruction serves merely to challenge and disrupt the *status quo*. The question of what comes after it, of how social arrangements ought to be transformed so as to better approximate social justice is dismissed, if not greeted with outright hostility. For this is the modernist project, which presupposes norms of rationality and morality around which to forge consensus. But such norms are totally ungrounded and, worse, when promoted by the powers that be, are also inherently oppressive (Ellsworth, 1992; Lyotard, 1987).

Catharine MacKinnon (1989) likens this brand of deconstruction to a "neo-Cartesian mind game" (p. 137) that goes nowhere politically, if not backwards. For it "raises acontextualized interpretive possibilities that have no real social meaning or real possibility of any, thus dissolving the ability to criticize the oppressiveness of actual meanings" (1989, p. 137). Like Descartes, this kind of deconstruction embraces "hyperskepticism" (Barber, 1992) as its starting point, but, unlike Descartes, it finds no "clear and distinct" moorings for knowledge. Indeed, it finds no moorings at all.

Transformationists (among whom I include MacKinnon and Barber) charge that insofar as the aim of this kind of deconstruction embraces the political goal of eradicating oppression, it undermines its own political project.[3] This kind of deconstructivist activity renders the question of who the "terrorized" Others on the margins might be unanswerable (if not unaskable), for the reality of these Others as Others evaporates under the hot lights of deconstruction. Transformationists concede that identities aren't rigidly fixed and that prescribing a particular voice for members of marginalized groups can be condescending, stereotyping, and oppressive. As Henry Louis Gates remarks regarding the feeling he gets from his white colleagues in the academy: it is as if they were to provide him with a script and say, "Be oppositional—please. You look so cute when you're angry" (1992, chap. 10, p. 185). But Gates also warns against taking this observation too far. He writes:

> Foucault says, and let's take him at his word, that the "homosexual" as life form was invented sometime in the 19th century. Now, if there's no such thing as a homosexual, then homophobia, at least as directed toward people rather than acts, loses its rationale. But you can't respond to the discrimination against gay people by saying, "I'm sorry, I don't exist; you've got the wrong guy." (1992, chap. 2, pp. 37-38)

Gates uses this example to identify a tension between what he calls "the imperatives of agency" and "the rhetoric of dismantlement" (what I have been calling "deconstruction"). One can conceive of homosexuality (or race, or gender) as "*only* a sociopolitical category," as Gates puts it. But, consistent with my observations in the previous section, that does not mean that such social categories ("constructions") do not exist or are not real in their effects. Acknowledging that members of social groups do not necessarily speak with one voice, acknowledging that identity is, as Cameron McCarthy (1993) puts it, "nonsynchronous," transformationists are on their guard to avoid sliding into the sort of radical deconstruction of group identity Gates warns against, in which all that remains are decentered, radically unstable individuals.

The flip side of the transformationists' worry about the inability of radical deconstruction to make sense out of oppression is its inability to provide any guidance regarding how to educate persons so that they will be moral agents who can, among other things, recognize oppression and work against it. Daniel Dennett (1991), who rejects the Cartesian—or *modernist*—conception of the self in favor of what he calls a postmodernist conception, acknowledges the moral-political dangers in doing so. He thus embraces the idea of getting beyond a merely deconstructive activity to the activity of shaping selves of the right kind. Responding to an imagined interlocutor, Dennett writes:

> I think I know what you're getting at. If a self isn't a real thing, what happens to moral responsibility? One of the most important roles of self in our traditional conceptual schemes is as the place where the buck stops, as Harry Truman's sign announced. If selves aren't real—aren't *really* real—won't the buck just get passed on and on, round and round, forever? .... The task of constructing a self that can *take* responsibility is a major social and educational project ... (pp. 429-430)

Burbules (1996) makes a point similar to Dennett's when he observes that education is inherently about growth and development and is therefore inherently goal-directed. If Dennett and Burbules are right (and one could invoke Dewey and his notion of "growth" as well), it follows that however cautious educators can and ought to be about the norms, dispositions, attitudes, and knowledge they foster, foster some they must. In short, educators and educational researchers alike are required to engage in a *constructive* political activity.

Perhaps acknowledgment of this point explains why postmodernists in education are, by comparison to postmodernists more generally, relatively unabashed about embracing the project of ending oppression (but see Usher and Edwards, 1994). In any case, postmodern educationists are unable to consistently confine themselves only to deconstruction, and, whatever their avowals, they opt for transformation in the end.

Consider the following remark by Elisabeth Ellsworth:

> [I]n a classroom in which "empowerment" is made dependent on rationalism, those perspectives that would question the political interests (sexism, racism, colonialism, for example) expressed and guaranteed by rationalism would be rejected as "irrational" (biased, partial). (1992, p. 98)

But what is the alternative to "rationalism?" As Benjamin Barber asks:

> How can ... reformers think they will empower the voiceless by proving that voice is always a function of power? ... How do they think the struggle for equality and justice can be waged with an epistemology that denies standing to reasons and normative rational terms ....? (1992, p. 123)

Barber adds: "The powerful toy with reason, the powerless need it, for by definition it is their only weapon" (p. 124).

It would seem there is no way for those who would reject rationalism *carte blanche* to adequately respond to Barber's challenge. In the end, some overarching (and presumably "modernist") principle or principles must be embraced

(Burbules & Rice, 1991). And Ellsworth does exactly this when she proffers the following question as the "final arbiter" for determining the "acceptability" of anti-racist actions:

> To what extent do our political strategies and alternative narratives about social difference succeed in alleviating campus racism, while at the same time managing not to undercut the efforts of other social groups to win self-definition? (1992, p. 110)

Isn't this a principle guiding political action? Doesn't it have a specific goal? Isn't it (shouldn't it be, can't it be) rationally agreed to?

Some self-described postmodernist educationists explicitly embrace general political principles. For example, Stanley Aronowitz and Henry Giroux (1991) acknowledge the force of the general sort of criticism advanced by Barber. In response, they call for a "critical" (versus "apolitical") postmodernism in which the "postmodern politics of difference" is combined with the "modernist struggle for justice, equality, and freedom" (p. 194).

Here we see the line (or "border") between postmodernists and transformationists explicitly crossed. For "critical postmodernism" cannot be systematically distinguished from the so-called meta-narratives of Marxism and liberalism that it putatively rejects. The "modernist struggle" continues for Marxism and liberalism, and neither tradition has remained static. On the contrary, both have evolved so as to better cope with the "politics of difference," so emphasized in postmodernist analyses.[4]

As I acknowledged at the outset, there are dangers in trying to divide philosophical stances taken toward the interpretive turn into postmodernist and transformationist. This should be even more evident in light of the preceding several paragraphs. In educational theory at least, various views seem to fall on a continuum regarding the degree to which they embrace transformation. Very few shun transformation altogether.

Those I have been calling postmodernists tread very lightly. They are highly tentative about speaking for others and categorizing them, about what to do in the wake of deconstruction, and are highly suspicious of those who claim to know what is best. They also emphasize paying very close attention to one's own social position and "subjectivities." Those I have been calling transformationists do not ignore these concerns, but they are less guarded. They proceed by identifying oppressed groups and by articulating and employing broad political principles—justice, equality, and the like—to criticize existing conditions and to suggest the direction that transformations should take.

Ellsworth, as well as Aronowitz and Giroux, emphasize curriculum, pedagogy and politics, but the same point can be made with respect to educational research. Consider Patti Lather's book *Getting Smart* (1991a). The subtitle, *Feminist Research and Pedagogy With/in Postmodernism*, as well as much of her exposition and vocabulary, suggest she is advancing a straightforward postmodernist approach to educational research, to be distinguished from a modernist (or Enlightenment) one. But Lather explicitly denies that she embraces thoroughgoing deconstructionism (and its nihilistic consequences); she would limit deconstruction to opening up space for the expression of hitherto silenced voices. In this connection, she repeatedly and approvingly cites the work of critical theorist Brian Fay (1975, 1987), whose project is clearly a transformational one (however guarded and qualified).

In general, interpretivist educational research jettisons the positivist goal of "technical control" (Howe, 1992). Various ends (academic achievement and increased economic competitiveness, for instance) cannot be bracketed and set to one side while educational researchers go about the task of investigating the best means of achieving them, with an eye toward exerting more effective control. Ends must be left on the table, as not ultimately separable from means, and as themselves being an important part of what needs to be investigated and negotiated. Postmodernists and transformationists are in substantial agreement to this point. They diverge from here, however, and their respective responses to the demise of the positivist fact/value dichotomy may be used to illustrate how.

The fact/value dichotomy is shorthand for a much more inclusive set of distinctions. On the fact side, it also puts rationality, science, means, cognition, objectivity, and truth. On the value side, it also puts irrationality, politics, ends, interests, subjectivity and power. Postmodernists focus on the value side, which engulfs the fact side. Thus, we get the picture (in Foucault, for instance) that science, truth, and the like are simply masks for power. Alternatively, transformationists *blend* the fact and value sides. Thus, we get the picture (in Habermas, for instance) that although science and truth can be corrupted— "distorted"—by power, they are nonetheless redeemable if checked by the kind of rationality associated with an emancipatory interest.

But here again the difference between postmodernists and transformationists (at least in education) may be overdrawn. Assume that postmodernists do, indeed, embrace the goal of ending oppression. This puts them in some general agreement with transformationists. Nonetheless, they may still complain that transformationists are far too confident both in how they understand this goal and the means by which it can be best achieved. It is *they*—the transformationists— who have a self-defeating project that oppresses through its overconfident paternalism.

In my view, this sort of disagreement can but does not have to turn on fundamental philosophical incompatibilities. It may turn on *practical* questions like: When should I bite my tongue? What's the best way to move things along? What would be the long-term consequences of intervening now? How can I get these people to see what's really going on here? And other questions like: What's my stake in this? Have I failed to appreciate what's being said? Who am I to interpret this situation by my lights? And so on. Consider these questions in light of the practice of "female circumcision." Now, consider them in light of what we know about public schools' treatment of girls, people of color, and gay, lesbian, and bisexual youth. I am suggesting that, whether they *have* done so or not, postmodernists and transformationists *could* end up answering these questions in much the same way. They could end up agreeing that taking action in a certain set of circumstances would be ill-advised; they could end up agreeing that action should be taken but in the form of some tentative first steps; and so forth.

Conclusion: Toward Closing the New Divides

In the wake of the interpretive turn, the philosophical debate is now between those who seek some new understandings of knowledge, rationality, truth, and objectivity (i.e., transformationists) and those who seem ready to abandon these as hopelessly wedded to the bankrupt modernist project (i.e., postmodernists).

But this may well draw the line too sharply. For the specific disagreements between postmodernists and transformationists—on epistemology, ontology, and politics—may be largely practical. In any case, there seem to be three general points of agreement. First, "subjectivities" count. This is a general implication of the interpretive turn and the constructivist epistemology that goes with it. Second, social arrangements are irremediably interest-, power- and value-laden. Accordingly, they need to be carefully examined—"deconstructed"—in this light. And third, the end result of educational research and practice should be transformation to a more just and democratic system of schooling and, ultimately, a more just and democratic society.

To be sure, differences between postmodernists and transformationists are significant. But if I am right, interpretivists of all stripes embrace both "deconstruction" and "transformation." They would do well to avoid overblowing their differences on how to understand and balance these in a way that engenders a new generation of paradigm cliques.

Notes

1 Some feminists are postmodernists, but many belong in the transformationist camp, for example, Seyla Benhabib, Iris Marion Young, Catharine MacKinnon, Lorraine Code, Sandra Harding, and Nancy Frazer, to name a few.

2 Although I find much of Searle's analysis useful, I do not embrace his realist view and believe his views on social reality do not depend on it.

3 For an elaboration of this argument, see also Bernstein (1996), Benhabib (1995), Gutmann (1994), Lyon (1994), and Taylor (1994).

4 Numerous examples exist in political theory, but for specific applications of critical theory to education see Robert Young and Nicholas Burbules (1993). For an application of liberalism see Kenneth Howe (1997).

Chapter 6

THE CONSTRUCTIVIST TURN

The idea of "constructivism" now pervades the educational research literature, where it is used to refer to three different things: learning theory, pedagogical theory, and epistemology. In this chapter, I will venture into each of these three areas. But the primary focus will be on constructivism as epistemology, consistent with the general themes of this book.

In the previous chapter I identified constructivism with interpretivism. Arguably, constructivism and interpretivism amount to the same thing, or at least stand in a relationship of mutual entailment. But for the purposes of this chapter I can make do with the weaker claim that there are close parallels between the "constructivist turn," as I shall call it, and the interpretive turn.

First, the constructivist turn, like the interpretive turn, results from abandoning "foundationalist" epistemology, and especially positivist epistemology. Knowledge is construed as actively constructed by human agents, rather than as passively received by them. Second, also like the interpretive turn, two general responses to the abandonment of positivism may be identified: "radical" constructivism and "social" constructivism. The former focuses heavily on the individual in knowledge construction; the latter, on social groups. Third, and like the interpretive turn in yet another way, the radical versus social constructivist split raises some of the same fundamental issues concerning subjectivity and relativism as the postmodernist versus transformationist split.

The remainder of this chapter is divided into four major sections. The first is called *Constructivism's Kantian Roots*. This bit of history is worth undertaking for two general reasons. First, "epistemology" is a much over-worked term these days, so much so that it is often difficult to discern the difference between embracing a different epistemology—something quite fundamental and far reaching—and merely embracing different beliefs. Clarity is to be gained by examining constructivism in terms of the traditional philosophical sense of epistemology, as a general theory of knowledge. Second, "construct-ivism" is not prominent in the history of philosophy, though it has made an appearance of late.[1] The general idea has a relatively long history in philosophy, however, but has been associated with labels such as Kantianism, pragmatism, and naturalism. Getting clear on what counts as constructivist epistemology may be facilitated by first getting clear on the basic contours of several important epistemological views in the history of Western philosophy, as well as certain problems these views encountered.

The second section is called *Constructivism and the Linguistic Turn*. This section is the most extended of the chapter. It describes how, beginning in the 20th century, language became central in the analysis of knowledge production and expression. I describe the general view that I call "post-Kantianism" and how it was manifested in the epistemology of science, including social science.

The third section is the *Foundering of Radical Constructivism*. It provides a critique of "radical constructivism," a view that is markedly individualistic and that is typically contrasted with "social constructivism." (The latter includes post-Kantianism).

The fourth and concluding section is called *Toward a Thoroughgoing Constructivism*. Here I very briefly characterize constructivist learning and pedagogical theories and suggest how they might be integrated with a constructivist epistemology to form a thoroughgoing constructivist conception of educational research.

Constructivism's Kantian Roots

In the sense that the mind is implicated in some way in determining what the world is, all epistemological views are constructivist, a point made well by Phillips (1995). So "constructivism" must pick out something sufficient to distinguish it from other epistemological views.

Two non- (or halfway) constructivist epistemologies have dominated in the history of Western philosophy: empiricism and rationalism. In empiricism, all knowledge is grounded in experience. The mind passively receives experience and is active in knowledge construction only *post hoc*, as it were, only in the sense of ordering what is already *given* in experience. In rationalism, by contrast, the mind is the starting place for knowledge, and it is also implicated in the experience of the empirical world. Consider Descartes' famous wax example. How is it, asks Descartes, that a melting piece of wax can undergo changes in shape, color, and other sensible qualities and yet remain the same piece of wax? His answer is that the mind discerns "substance," a substrate behind the sensible qualities of the wax that makes it the same thing through its sensible changes.

Empiricism and rationalism faced different kinds of problems. Empiricists were faced with the difficulty of making sense of experience as totally detached from the contribution of the mind. For if the mind were altogether passive in experience, how could experience organize *itself* into the chairs, the sky, the electrons, the persons, and so forth, that minds experience? Related to this, if a mind were not something distinct from a mere bundle of experiences, how could it persist as a thing over time that has experiences? Wouldn't it be nothing but a sequence of ever changing minds as it (whatever *it* refers to) received new experiences over time? Wouldn't it become something different each time its experiential contents changed?

Rationalists had an answer. Descartes proposed that the mind itself is a special kind of "substance" that exists independent of its experiential contents. But this engenders a different problem: If the mind operates autonomously, guided only by its own rules, how is a coherent connection established between reason and experience? Consider Zeno's famous paradoxes. Reason allegedly tells us that Achilles cannot cross the stadium. He must first traverse half the distance, then half the remaining distance, then half the remaining distance, and so on, *ad infinitum*, such that there will always be some remainder. Viewed from the other end of the sequence, Achilles not only cannot cross the stadium, he cannot move at all. Zeno, the rationalist, took this to be a victory. For, in his view, it shows that experience cannot be trusted.

The alternative to Zeno's conclusion, of course, is that it is the reasoning here that cannot be trusted. Why? Because it conflicts with common experience. On this alternative view, if reason is to be more than just a set of formal rules that have nothing to do with experience, then reason and experience have to somehow be brought in line with one another.

Enter Kant's attempted synthesis of empiricism and rationalism. To paraphrase one of Kant's leading ideas: a conceptual scheme without sensory data is empty, sensory data without a conceptual scheme are blind. This idea has to rank among the most influential and prescient in the history of Western philosophy—and it ushered in the true sense of constructivist epistemology.

Kant's view exemplifies a true constructivist view because it is more thoroughgoing than the halfway variants of empiricism and rationalism: it denies that there can be any *raw* sensory experience that the mind takes as given and then performs its formal operations on (empiricism). Alternatively, conceptual schemes are not pure (rationalism), but have meaning only as they are put to work in *constructing* experience. This mixing of the empirical and the conceptual, as it were, was not individual/subjective for Kant. Rather, the mental categories of space, time, causation, and enduring objects ("substance"), among others, were the preconditions of experience, the furniture of *all* minds.

In the twentieth century, language supplanted the role played by Kant's transcendental (and somewhat mysterious) categories. Wittgenstein, who I consider extensively in the next section, exemplifies the parallel. The important historical point to note about Kant's view is that constructivism was born in reaction to the two halfway constructivisms of empiricism and rationalism—and also born intersubjectivist.

Constructivism and the "Linguistic Turn"

Twentieth century constructivist epistemology may be approached from two general directions: (1) post-Kantianism and (2) the assault on positivism. The first pertains to epistemology generally, whereas the second focuses more on the epistemology of science. The two are intimately related insofar as each *naturalizes* epistemology by detaching knowledge from a transcendent realm and locating it, instead, in the natural phenomenon of language.

Post-Kantianism

Kant asked the question, How is experience as we know it possible? He then deduced categories like (Euclidean) space, cause and effect, enduring object ("substance") and the like. These categories are not themselves experienced because they are presupposed by experience from the start.

Wittgenstein asked a similar question: How is language use and learning possible? Like Kant, he didn't start from a given in the traditional sense— some self-certifying sense data or autonomous revelations of reason—but with a familiar fact about the world that must be accounted for. Also like Kant, he was neither an empiricist nor a rationalist in the classical senses described above. Finally, insofar as he may be attributed with having advanced an epistemological thesis, it was constructivist.[2]

Individuals are born, or "thrown" into linguistic communities (e.g., Young, 1990c). The linguistic resources and practices available, and which they have no choice about whether to learn, are saturated with cultural, historical, and social dimensions. And in order for someone to learn a language, both through instruction and more informally, the practices and concepts they encounter must exhibit consistency. Imagine the parent of a toddler points to a ball on one occasion and calls it a peach, then points to it on another occasion and calls it a parrot, then on a third occasion calls it a rhinoceros, then calls it a glacier, and so forth. The child is never going to learn what objects count as balls (or, incidentally, learn what pointing means either).

This all seems obvious enough, but Wittgenstein drew some profound conclusions from the starting point of humdrum linguistic practice. Against empiricism especially, he criticized the idea that linguistic constructions correspond to raw, "private" experiences, out of which is then built up knowledge. For Wittgenstein, there can be no raw sensory experiences—"experiencing ball now," "experiencing happy feeling now"—that exist prior to linguistic constructions and to which linguistic constructions are only later attached. Rather, the meanings of "ball" and "being happy" are inherent in, part-and-parcel of, language learning and use. Wittgenstein coined the term "language game" as a way of pointing to the rule-governed nature of linguistic practices and to the manner in which people catch on to the rules by actively engaging in such practices.

As I observed before, "constructivism" did not enter the philosophical lexicon until recently. One place it has been used consistently, however, is in reference to Wittgenstein's philosophy of mathematics. His view of mathematical truth is that it grows out of and cannot be separated from human activity. This is *constructivism* in the broad sense that goes just as easily under the name of *naturalism*. Naturalism denies any non- or super-natural criterion of truth, in contrast with the rationalist and non-constructivist view (e.g., Plato's) that mathematical knowledge is about a universal and timeless reality that is revealed by reason alone and whose features are totally independent of human experiences and activities.

Wittgenstein applies his brand of constructivism across the board, to also include epistemologically central concepts such as knowledge, doubt, and justification. He warns against "subliming" these concepts and turning them into "super concepts." Their meanings, no less than the meanings of more work-a-day concepts, are to be found in how they function in their "original homes," i.e., existing linguistic practices or "language games." So, for example, when Descartes begins the analysis of knowledge by doubting everything, including his own existence, Wittgenstein demands to know what the grounds for such a doubt could be. His point is that certain rules govern how doubt functions as a concept, including that there be some grounds for doubt. If one can doubt everything, including that one doubts, then the whole "game" falls apart.

To reiterate, Wittgenstein's naturalized epistemological constructivism eschews a given in the traditional sense. The ultimate justification for knowledge claims is what we say and do, our "form of life." Wittgenstein famously remarked on the logic of justification that it "... comes to an end. If it did not, it would not be justification" (1958, p. 132e). Further, "If I have exhausted the justifications I have reached bedrock ... Then I am inclined to say: 'This is simply what I do'" (1958, p. 85e).

Wittgenstein's general epistemological position is that it is fruitless, or worse, to seek any points of reference—"foundations"—for knowledge wholly outside the natural world, of which humankind is a part. Such a view—"anti-foundationalism" as it is often called—is by no means confined to Wittgenstein. The general contours of this view have come to dominate in the latter half of the 20th century.

My primary focus in this chapter is on explicating constructivist epistemology, not defending it. Nonetheless, a few observations are in order about the *conventionalism* that constructivist epistemology is allegedly committed to, and the problem of relativism that goes with it. What I have to say in this connection will help set the stage for the next section.

"The world as we know it bears the stamp of our own conceptual activity," Putnam says (1990, p. 261). Those who would criticize this kind of constructivist view find it worrisome (if not disastrous) that it allegedly renders truth contingent on the conventions of linguistic communities. The criterion of truth on such a view, or so it is argued, amounts to nothing more than agreement (if only tacit) among the members of such communities. But what if the members of such communities disagree amongst themselves? Can't the minority be right? Are there then no truths to be found? Are there many truths, each relative to those who hold them? And what if the members of a given community agree amongst themselves but disagree with the members of a different community?

This is a challenge toward which epistemological constructivists can ill-afford to be sanguine. They can ill-afford to simply capitulate, to say, "Yes, truths are *merely* matters of agreement," or "Yes, they're merely constructions." For this dooms epistemological constructivists to a radical and untenable form of relativism in which each individual constructs her own world.

One response by epistemological constructivists is to deny that it makes sense to claim truth merely amounts to convention by examining how the concept of truth operates in ordinary usage. When someone makes a claim of the general form "X is true," they are not claiming that this is something everyone in fact agrees to. That people agreed to X would be a separate claim, the truth of which would not necessarily affect whether X is indeed true. For example, when Copernicus claimed the earth revolves about the sun, he was not appealing to conventional belief. On the contrary, he was trying to change it. The convention governing truth is that truth is not a matter of convention! This point goes back to Wittgenstein's advice about not subliming epistemological concepts, in this case "truth," ignoring how they function in their "original home" of human practices. A similar stance toward the concept of truth is to be found in pragmatists and neo-pragmatists such as James, Dewey, Putnam, and Rorty.

But isn't this just sleight of hand? "The *real* problem," critics are likely to rejoin, "is that epistemological constructivism has no criteria outside of what people say and do to determine the truth. *This* is the sense of conventionalism that leads to a disastrous relativism." Invoked implicitly here is a fundamental *Either-Or*: *Either* there exists some wholly external, extra-human world by which to verify knowledge claims, *Or* truth resides solely in what individuals and groups construct, i.e., in their conventions. It is the latter disjunct that epistemological constructivists are attributed with embracing, and it is because these constructions/conventions don't have to hook up with the world that relativism is the ineluctable result.

The response of epistemological constructivists is not to provide a solution to the question of how the world hooks up with mind/language. Rather, they reject this question as fruitless and misguided, because based on an untenable dualism between the world and humans' constructions of it. If there is no rigid demarcation between these two things, then there is no sense worrying about whether the two hook up. They have to. This stance of post-Kantian constructivists is exemplified well by Putnam:

> [E]lements of what we call "language" or "mind" *penetrate so deeply into what we call reality that the very project of representing ourselves as "mappers" of something "language-independent" is fatally compromised from the very start . . . ".* In this situation it is a temptation to say, "So we make the world," or "our language makes up the world," or "our culture makes up the world;" but this is just another form of the same mistake. (1990, p. 28)

The Constructivist Assault on Positivism

In philosophy of science, the twentieth century "linguistic turn" saw classical empiricism rejuvenated as logical positivism. Once again a wedge was driven between the empirical and the conceptual—the world and our constructions of it—just as in classical empiricism. On the other hand, logical positivism relativized the distinction to language. Rather than setting minds and their ideas over and against experiences, the logical positivists set formal logic over and against observation sentences. Observation sentences served as conceptually neutral building blocks that were organized by formal logic and from which predictions and explanations were deduced. Like its forerunner, classical empiricism, logical positivism was a halfway constructivist view.

The twentieth century also saw constructivism rejuvenated. At least as important as the developments described in the previous section (and not unrelated to them) were important developments in philosophy of science. Paralleling the place Wittgensteinian "language games" occupied in the analysis of knowledge in general, Quinean "conceptual schemes" and Kuhnian "paradigms" assumed a prominent place in the analysis of scientific knowledge in particular.

Notions such as conceptual schemes and paradigms exemplify a constructivist view because they are characterized in a way that precludes abstracting the purely linguistic from the purely empirical and setting the two over and against one another. Contrary to logical positivism, observation is always "theory-laden"—the basic empirical building blocks of knowledge are laden with conceptual content at birth.

To be sure, a certain form of the relativism, namely, relativity to conceptual schemes or paradigms, threatens the Quinean-Kuhnian account. Insofar as this threat is based on the same dualism between language/mind and the world discussed in the previous section, it may be dismissed in the same way. Indeed, the denial of this dualism is central to Quine's (1962) seminal critique of positivism. In any case, the kind of relativism associated with Quine and Kuhn is a far cry from the radical, individualistic version found in "radical constructivism." For there remains a good deal of room for truth, objectivity, and rationality within communities that share conceptual schemes and paradigms because such communities inherently incorporate standards that serve as the basis for their identities and for intersubjective judgments among their members. Indeed, one of Kuhn's major points is the social and socializing character of scientific paradigms.

Furthermore, although moves from one conceptual scheme or paradigm to another cannot be characterized in terms of a set of mechanically applied rules and are not straightforwardly cumulative, such scientific "revolutions" or "paradigm shifts," as Kuhn calls them, are not therefore based on private, subjective beliefs. The shared problems, vocabulary, and methodological canons specific to a given area of scientific endeavor loom large in dealing with anomalous findings. Even where major theoretical upheaval—scientific "revolution"—is on the horizon, the old paradigm, although not straightforwardly subsumable under the new (this is the positivist account of scientific progress), nonetheless overlaps significantly (Kuhn, 1977). In general, whether revolutionary or more modest theory revision is at issue, overarching "values" (as Kuhn, 1977, calls them) or "pragmatic criteria" (as Quine, 1970, calls them) apply intersubjectively so as to markedly circumscribe what theories ("constructions") are viable candidates and to determine which among them wins out. Among these values or criteria are consistency, coherence, scope, simplicity, and explanatory power.

The Quinean-Kuhnian alternative to positivism, then, does not go so far in repudiating positivism as to jettison truth, scientific rationality, and objectivity. On the contrary, it reinterprets these concepts in a way that dispenses with the kind of pristine observational basis for science associated with positivism and, especially in Kuhn's work, seeks to bring them into line with the history of theoretical advances. On this account, scientific progress proceeds by a kind of bootstrapping that Kuhn (1962) likens to Darwinian evolution: new theories are compared to those they seek to displace in terms of their fitness *vis-à-vis* the existing problematic and the kinds of general pragmatic criteria described above, rather than to some criterion to which science must inexorably move. Importantly, however, rationality, objectivity, and truth seeking remain hallmarks of the scientific enterprise. These are inherently intersubjective. As such, they constrain what individual "constructors" can come up with, as well as how what they come up with is to be judged.

In addition to natural science, 20th century philosophy of social science, too, moved toward constructivism. Logical positivism gained a strong foothold in social science, and it also came in for intense criticism there.

Positivism's commitment to a neutral observation language was doubly problematic when it came to investigating human behavior. The vocabulary of social science is conceptually laden in the same way that it is in natural science. But in addition, the objects (subjects) it attempts to conceptualize are themselves conceptualizers. Understanding human behavior requires that various perspectives be included in, as Helen Longino (1993) puts it, a "critical knowledge-constructive dialogue." Understanding the behavior of sub-atomic particles requires no similar kind of dialogue.

Thus, "constructivism" comes closer to being a literal description of the currently ascendant epistemology of social science than of the philosophy of natural science or of epistemology generally. For example, in his suggestively titled *The Construction of Social Reality*, John Searle (1995) contends that human behavior must be understood against a "background of intentionality." The basic idea here is that, unlike in the case of physical objects, the description and explanation of human behavior requires appeal to human purposes that, in turn, can only be interpreted within a system of shared norms that determine what counts as what. For example, saying certain things, with certain purposes, under certain conditions constitutes getting married. By contrast, merely moving in certain ways and emitting certain noises—a physical description of events— does not by itself entail a marriage has occurred. Neither does doing all the typically right things, but in the context of a play. In both cases the movements, noises, and situation must be interpreted against a background of shared meanings. And what distinguishes *these* meanings from those in the natural sciences is that they have to be known from the inside, from the interpretive-constructivist point of view of the actors themselves.

Still, even in the case of social reality, "constructivism" shouldn't be taken too literally. As a rule, individuals do not reflect on and actively construct the social meanings that govern their lives. As I observed before, they are "thrown" into a network of such meanings—a network that, for the most part, has not been deliberately constructed. Through their on-going participation in social activities, individuals master the typically unarticulated and tacitly conveyed "know hows" (Searle, 1995) of social life. Only against such large and complex background of *shared social constructions* can they consciously reflect and evaluate social life.

Once again, relativism raises its head, and it appears more acute in the case of knowledge about social reality than in the case of knowledge about physical reality. Constructions of social reality, even though unavoidably shared to a large degree *within* groups, vary *among* groups. Because various systems of shared norms and purposes may be judged good or bad, an additional kind of relativism arises in the case of social reality, namely, moral relativism.

Once again, the challenge of relativism has to be taken seriously, and the kind of responses that constructivism can provide to it parallels the ones offered before. First, it won't do to say, "Yes, morality is *merely* a matter of agreement," or "Yes, morality is *merely* a construction." For "X is right (or wrong)" is no more a claim about what people in fact agree to than "X is true" is. Both are general claims for which argument and evidence have to be marshaled and, to hold up, such claims must withstand counter arguments and evidence. In this vein, Sandra Harding (1993) denies that "descriptive relativism"—groups X, Y, and Z hold different moral beliefs—implies "judgmental relativism"—groups X, Y, Z, are each correct in their moral beliefs.

Second, just as epistemological constructivism denies the dualism between mind/language and the world, it denies the dualism between values and the world. As Putnam says, "without *values* we would not have a *world*" (1990, p.141). Epistemological constructivism puts ethical values—justice, goodness, rightness—on the same footing with cognitive values—coherence, scope, explanatory power—such that both "penetrate" the world. Disagreement about interpretation, application, and relative importance cannot be eliminated in either case. Putnam concludes: "if . . . ethical values are totally subjective, then cognitive values are totally subjective as well" (1990, p. 140). Though certain postmodernists may be prepared to draw the conclusion that both morality and science are subjective to the core, epistemological constructivism, as conceived here, draws the conclusion that neither is.

The Foundering of Radical Constructivism

Radical constructivism starts with individuals' private constructions of reality. Everything else must be built up from there. This is interestingly reminiscent of classical empiricism, and suffers from the same problems.[3] For example, how can research get a toehold if research participants are all busy constructing their own private worlds? And what could the grounds be for getting an account of the social world right?

It seems that the only way to adequately address these questions is in terms of a shared world, made up of shared meanings. Yet radical constructivists challenge the notion of shared meanings. According to von Glasersfeld, the belief that meanings or knowledge are held in common among different individuals can be more or less "viable" but not true (at least not in terms of philosophers' conception of "truth"). Borrowing an expression from Paul Cobb, von Glasersfeld (1996) contends that allegedly shared meanings are really only "taken-as-shared" and only "seem compatible." He writes:

> The conceptual structures that constitute meanings or knowledge are not entities that could be used alternatively by different individuals. They are constructs that each user has to build up for him- or herself. And because they are individual constructs, one can never say whether or not two people have produced the same construct. At best one may observe that in a given number of situations their constructs seem to function in the same way, that is, seem compatible.
>
> That is why those who are stressing the social dimension of language would do well to use Paul Cobb's expression "taken-as-shared" . . . (1996, p. 5)

The bridge between the subjective and the intersubjective is built by "imputing" shared meanings. The private worlds of the researcher and research participants are "taken-as-shared." Thus, the researcher proceeds *as if* there is a world of shared meanings to be revealed.

This is a shaky bridge indeed, in serious danger of collapsing at several points. For doesn't replacing "shared meanings" with meanings that are "taken as shared" just push the question back a step? Do we share a meaning for "taken as shared" or is the meaning of "taken as shared" merely "taken as shared?" If the latter, is *that* merely "taken as shared?" How can radical constructivists talk to one another? Worse, how can they talk to themselves? Are von Glasersfeld's meanings on Monday the same as his meanings on Friday, or does he merely take them to be the same? How could he know?

The earlier discussion of Wittgenstein's views on the preconditions of language learning are pertinent here, and may be expanded somewhat to seriously call into question using the notion of "taken-as-shared" as the bridge between private worlds of meaning and a shared world. For individuals construct meanings within a community into which they have been "thrown" in the way described previously. The meanings they construct—master and learn to employ—come to them already saturated with what the community shares as a community. Recall the example of the child learning the meaning of "ball." Does this child merely take it as shared, *assume*, her parent means the same thing by pointing that she does? Is this assumption one the child consciously makes—"I assume when Mommy motions that way she's pointing, not hailing a cab." This is pretty far fetched, particularly for a child at the rudimentary stage of language learning, who has not mastered the "language game" of assuming.

To be sure, there is a sense in which accomplished language users assume that people share meanings with them. However—and this is the crux—public, intersubjective criteria are required to show when this assumption is violated. If not, if each individual lived in a privately constructed world, accessible only to her- or himself, what grounds could there ever be for *not* taking meanings as shared? For example, if Susan calls a lion a tiger and Johnny says the square root of 9 is 4 1/2, why shouldn't I continue to take their *meanings* (as opposed to their *words for them*) as shared with mine? Why isn't this just as warranted as the conclusion we don't share meanings? After all, I have no access to their private worlds. So, for all I can know, Susan means by "tiger" what I mean by "lion" and Johnny means by "4 1/2" what I mean by "3."

It is much more sensible to embrace a world of shared—or public—meanings. In it there is a correct class of referents for "tiger" and a correct answer to the question "What's the square root of 9?" and Susan's and Johnny's behavior tell me that they don't know what these are. And the response to Susan and Johnny, particularly if I'm their teacher, is to correct their mistaken beliefs. "No Susan, I can see why you might think that's a tiger, but it's a lion. Tigers have stripes." "No Johnny, but good try. 4 1/2 is what you get when you divide 9 by 2. The square root of 9 is the number that gives you 9 when you multiply it by itself, which is 3. Do you see? So, what's the square root of 25?"

A big part of the problem here is that radical constructivists conflate different *meanings of meaning*. Consider the meaning of "Grant Park." In one sense, it means a large park in Chicago, on the shore of Lake Michigan, site where protesters at the 1968 Democratic convention were beaten and teargassed, etc. In another sense—the sense in which a teacher might assign as an essay entitled "What Grant Park means to me"—the *meaning* of "Grant Park" is associated with personal experiences. In this sense, "Grant Park" *means* something very different to a person who was beaten and arrested than to someone who spent a lovely spring afternoon there. The important point is that we don't have to—and don't in fact—take this latter sense of meaning as shared. By contrast, the first sense isn't merely "taken as shared," but *has to be* shared for communication to be possible. Also, it is presupposed by the second kind of meaning. For example, if a student proceeded to write his essay "What Grant Park means to me" about Wrigley Field, he would have to be corrected, taught what the referent of "Grant Park" is.

These observations about shared meanings can be extended beyond the simple case of naming. Consider Charles Taylor's (1987) discussion of "constitutive meanings," as distinct from "common meanings." The latter refer to beliefs we largely share but that are not definitive of social life and activity, e.g., in chess it is bad strategy to move the Queen early. "Constitutive meanings" go deeper, however. In general, constitutive meanings must be shared in order for a vast array of human practices to be possible. The rules governing how the Queen may move provide a case in point. If one violates or ignores these rules such that the Queen was moved willy-nilly, or moved like a Knight, or what have you, then there would still be the activity of pushing pieces around on a board made of squares but it wouldn't be chess.

Similarly, suppose Horace writes "10, (=+4, 6)" on his arithmetic paper. Is this a mistaken construction or an idiosyncratic but nonetheless correct one? Perhaps it is a novel way of adding 4 and 6. Only further investigation could reveal whether this is true, and the results of such an investigation would depend on whether the attempt to systematically translate this string of symbols into some version of "(4+6)=10" was successful. Without this shared criterion, there simply would be no way to settle the question about whether Horace knows how to add.

In sum, radical constructivism provides no way for individuals to get beyond their privately constructed worlds. It is, indeed, caught in a hopelessly relativistic predicament.

Conclusion: Toward a Thoroughgoing Constructivism

There are certain parallels between the "interpretive turn" and the "constructivist turn." In each case, researchers abandon foundationalist epistemology and are then faced with the problem of how a view of knowledge grounded in interpretation-construction can avoid falling into relativism. On the one side are postmodernists and radical constructivists, who embrace relativism (or at least must live with it as anomalous). On the other side are transformationists and post-Kantian constructivists, who dismiss relativism as untenable.

The interpretive and constructivist turns diverge in one important respect. Whereas "interpretivism" has been used primarily to characterize a certain epistemology of social research, "constructivism" has been used primarily to characterize a certain psychology of learning and pedagogy. In my final remarks, I briefly suggest how a constructivist epistemology of social research and a constructivist psychology of pedagogy and learning might be more tightly drawn together to form a *thoroughgoing constructivism.*

Constructivist learning theory has its primary roots in the work of Piaget and Vygotsky. (It is by no means a stretch to claim that Dewey also held a constructivist theory of learning, indeed, in a rather carefully developed form.) Constructivist learning theory has two basic premises: (1) learning takes as its starting point the knowledge, attitudes, and interests students bring to the learning situation, and (2) learning results from the interaction between these characteristics and experience in such a way that learners *construct* their own understanding, from the inside.

As John Dewey (1938) observed, although simple in principle, constructivist learning theory is by no means simple to apply in instructional practice. On the contrary, because it requires knowing a good deal about students' starting points, it is much more demanding than subject-centered, authoritarian approaches to teaching. To further complicate matters, specific teaching techniques, for example, lecture versus Socratic dialogue versus collaborative learning, are not necessarily constructivist or not in relation to a more general pedagogical approach and epistemology.

Constructivist pedagogy is thus broader in scope than constructivist learning theory. It may be characterized as (1) embracing a constructivist learning theory, but (2) mixing ostensibly constructivist and non-constructivist teaching techniques as appropriate.

Dewey provided a foundation for such a constructivist pedagogy in constructivist epistemology (though his epistemological view was variously referred to as "instrumentalism," "experimentalism," and "pragmatism"). He advocated a holistic approach to curriculum and instruction, in which all subjects in the curriculum were to be integrated and subsumed under the overarching goal of promoting a truly democratic community. To be sure, Dewey's abiding commitment to democracy looms large here, but this commitment is by no means an isolated feature of his view. For it is also underpinned by a constructivist epistemology that is fallibilistic and dynamic, and that significantly blurs the boundaries between facts and science, on the one hand, and morals and politics, on the other. Complementing Dewey's epistemology is a pedagogy that spans the curriculum and that *begins* with what students value, believe, and have an interest in. If successful, it *ends* with having initiated students into the shared meanings—"experience *funded*," as William James (1968, p.71) put it—of a community, however subject to test and revision some of these may be.[4]

A general constructivist pedagogy along these Deweyan lines, then, requires fostering the moral and intellectual dispositions required of democratic citizenship, as well as other skills and knowledge (in natural science, mathematics, history, geography, etc.) needed for individuals to be in control of their lives and to be able to engage in fruitful and respectful dialogue with other members of the community. Such a pedagogical approach, it should be noted, is congenial to the burgeoning contemporary interest and scholarship in moral and political education exemplified by a diverse group of constructivists on the current scene, including radical pedagogues, feminists, and contemporary liberals.

A *thoroughgoing* epistemological constructivism would apply these same principles to educational research. It would be fundamentally participatory. It would *begin* with what stakeholders in education value, understand, and have an interest in. If successful, it would *end* with having initiated them into the shared meanings of genuine educational activity, however subject to test and revision some of these may be. It would avoid a radical constructivist stance that leaves knowledge ultimately trapped within privately constructed worlds.[5]

Notes

1 See, for example, Elgin (1997), Hacking (1999), and Searle (1995).

2 In an important sense Wittgenstein swears off the enterprise of epistemology as misguided. I call a view like Wittgenstein's *post*-epistemological in the next chapter.

3 See, for example, Garrison (1994), Gruender (1996), Matthews (1993), and Phillips (1995).

4 The constructivist movement is strikingly reminiscent of the progressive movement. Like constructivists, progressives set themselves in opposition to the prevailing authoritarian tradition in education. But (certain) progressives went too far. Reacting against the manner in which traditional educational arrangements invested authority almost exclusively in subject matter, they invested authority almost exclusively in students. Dewey was often associated with this so-called "child-centered" approach, but he actually disdained it as Either-Or thinking and likened it to "jumping out the frying pan into the fire." (Dewey, 1938, p. 64).

5 I revisit this topic in Chapter 9 in terms of "hyper-egalitarianism."

Chapter 7

ON THE THREAT OF EPISTEMOLOGICAL BIAS

An obstacle standing in the way of the kind of interpretivist-constructivist view elaborated in the preceding two chapters is the charge that any such view is inevitably *biased* and, consequently, inevitably involves foisting some dominant—and therefore oppressive— view of the world on marginalized people. I suggested in Chapter 5 that this charge suffers from internal inconsistency. That is, it presupposes some standpoint from which to identify and criticize oppressive relationships at the same time that it denies such a standpoint is defensible. In this chapter, I delve into this charge more deeply by examining the idea of *epistemological bias*—what it might mean and how it might be overcome.

I should be clear that my intention in is not to dismiss the idea of biased epistemology. As Janet Radcliff Richards observes, "If a group is kept out of doing something for long enough, it is overwhelmingly likely that . . . activities will develop in a way unsuited to the excluded group" (1980, pp. 113–114). There is no reason why this can't apply to epistemological investigation as much as to other kinds. So, insofar as epistemological theorizing has been an exclusionary activity, the idea of a biased epistemology is *prima facie* tenable.

But there are a number of complexities involved in cashing out this idea, both with respect to its precise meaning and with respect to its implications. Thus, in the next three sections I entertain three questions: What is bias? What is epistemology? and What is biased epistemology? In the final section I suggest that the *principle of inclusion* is a promising means by which the educational research community can control epistemological bias—and other forms of bias as well.

What is Bias?

Among the common synonyms for "biased" found in dictionary definitions are "prejudiced," "close-minded," "partial," "self-serving," "unreasonable," and "unfair." Thus, when someone says in response to another's claim, "That's a biased claim," they are criticizing the claim for suffering from one or more of the above faults. Bias is a bad thing for a belief, claim, or theory to be infected with, which is why social and educational researchers worry about how they can identify and avoid it, particularly in its more subtle and unconscious forms.

Notwithstanding the generally critical connotation of calling a claim biased, pronouncements like "all claims are biased" have become remarkably commonplace these days—as if bias was inevitable and thus not something to be troubled about. These once unorthodox pronouncements merit examination because they significantly muddy the meaning and implications of bias, if they don't render it utterly vacuous.

Wittgenstein observes in his *Philosophical Investigations* (1958) that if you followed every sentence with an exclamation point, pretty soon the meaning of exclamation points would be lost. You could just drop them off as superfluous, for they wouldn't serve to pick out any sentences as distinctive. Similarly, the notion of bias would be superfluous if it applied to all claims.

Consider the following assertions:

- The square of the hypotenuse equals the sum of the squares of the two adjacent sides.

- Slavery is an abomination.

- The earth is spherical.

- Steven Spielberg is overrated.

- School choice exacerbates inequities in public education.

It is hard to imagine (though I wouldn't confidently say unheard of) that someone would deny that the above list of assertions differ in the level of confidence that can be placed in their truth. Thus, "all claims are biased" might be interpreted less literally, to mean, "all claims are biased to *some degree*." So, we might say, "The square of the hypotenuse equals the sum of the squares of the two adjacent sides, that's the tiniest bit biased," and "Steven Spielberg is overrated, that's hugely biased." The interesting point here is that if we oppose "biased" to "objective" and start at the other end of the continuum, we get "all claims are objective to *some degree*." We also get, "The square of the hypotenuse equals the sum of the squares of the two adjacent sides, that's hugely objective," and "Steven Spielberg is overrated, that's the tiniest bit objective."

In the context of educational research, the descriptors "objective" and "biased" are used to evaluate claims in terms of the methodological procedures from which they have been derived. Thus, arguments about the warrant of controversial claims—for example, "School choice exacerbates inequities in public education"—often turn on procedural criteria. To say that a claim is objective is to say it has been arrived at by defensible procedures; to say that it is biased is to deny this. To be sure, there are number of complexities here (some of which I take up later). But if the notion of bias doesn't involve some criteria that determine when it may be correctly applied—if all claims are equally biased—we have no way of distinguishing claims in terms of whether, or the degree to which, they are biased. The fact that it is often difficult to make a determination doesn't imply that there is no difference between an objective claim and a biased one any more than dusk implies there is no difference between day and night.

To anticipate a bit of what is to come in the third section, the foregoing reasoning applies straightforwardly to the issue of epistemological bias. Here, too, we require criteria to determine whether, or the degree to which, claims of the form "E is a biased epistemology" are warranted. Otherwise, there is no way to determine whether "E is a biased epistemology" has any more or less going for it—or is any more or less biased—than "E is not a biased epistemology."

What is Epistemology?

References to "epistemology" and its cognates currently flood academic journals and books, including in educational research. It is probably a good thing that people are paying much greater attention to the epistemological underpinnings of educational research than they once did. But, as more and more people have joined the fray, "epistemology" has become significantly overworked and what counts as an epistemological question has become significantly blurred. As I observed in the last chapter, it has become difficult to discern the difference between groups of people embracing different epistemologies and merely embracing different beliefs.

The *Cambridge Dictionary of Philosophy* (Moser, 1995) defines epistemology as "the study of the nature of knowledge and justification." The key here is the reference to the "study of," for it helps bring into focus the fact that epistemology, a branch of philosophy, involves both articulating and evaluating conceptions of knowledge and justification. Put in another way, epistemology as the "study of . . . " has both a descriptive dimension—the epistemological principles that *are* employed by given communities—and a normative dimension—the epistemological principles that *ought to be* employed. For example, the epistemological presuppositions underlying so-called "quantitative" research may well be positivistic, at least for a fair number of researchers. It does not follow from this, however, that these researchers know the intricacies of positivist epistemology, much less that they have embraced it on the basis of a self-conscious epistemological investigation.

Thus, *epistemologies-in-use*[1]— the kinds of criteria and principles that groups in fact use in generating knowledge claims and justifications for them— are not epistemologies, strictly speaking, for they lack the self-conscious, normative element. This is not to disparage different "ways of knowing," necessarily, but to suggest that for something to count as an epistemological view, it must be self- consciously about knowledge and its justification. In this way, epistemology-in-use is similar to psychology-in-use. Examples of the latter include *folk* psychology as well as the kind of psychological presuppositions that are tacit in economic theory. Both epistemology-in-use and psychology-in-use should be distinguished from systematic, disciplined approaches to their subject matters.

The distinction between epistemology-in-use and epistemology more broadly conceived is reflected in the way epistemological investigation has historically proceeded. Epistemologists from Plato to the positivists have focused on the interplay between the descriptive and normative dimensions of knowledge. Plato sought to ground knowledge in transcendent Forms and to use these as the criterion for dismissing claims to knowledge based on mere *appearances*. Working in the other direction, the positivists' sought to ground knowledge in *neutral* observation and to use this as the criterion for dismissing claims to knowledge based on *metaphysics*. Despite the tremendous differences in what they took the foundations to be, both Plato and the positivists sought to develop normative criteria of knowledge which could serve as the basis upon which to evaluate knowledge claims in general, independent of the systems of beliefs and principles of justification that are, in fact, accepted and employed, and independent of the interests such beliefs and principles serve.[2]

This account of epistemology is significantly complicated by the fact that whether the distinction between its descriptive and normative elements can hold up is itself an epistemological question—a question about the nature and justification of knowledge. Nietzsche, for example, collapsed the normative into the descriptive by identifying knowledge claims with the will to power. Neo-Nietzschians such as Michel Foucault have refined and extended Nietzsche's thesis by developing the notion of "regimes of truth" and by describing how power flows through them so as to "normalize" people. For Nietzsche and Foucault, there are no non-contingent, normative criteria—Plato's Forms or the positivists' neutral observations, for instance—that provide the foundation for knowledge. Accordingly, there are no normative criteria of knowledge which can serve as the basis upon which to evaluate knowledge claims in general, independent of interests and of the systems of beliefs and principles of justification—"regimes of truth"—that are, in fact, accepted and employed.

Epistemological investigation (to the extent this is a serviceable notion at all) is limited to explicating—or "unmasking"—epistemologies-in-use.

Since about the mid twentieth century, the quest for the kind of foundations sought by Plato and the positivists has been largely abandoned. But this doesn't mean the normative/descriptive distinction has been abandoned as well. A general current of epistemological thought that may be termed *post*-epistemology has resisted conflating the normative and the descriptive in the way that *anti*-epistemologists such as Nietzsche and his successors do.

Post-epistemology is a view that may be attributed to thinkers such as Charles Taylor and Richard Rorty. For Taylor, this means overcoming the traditional "epistemological construal" (1995b); for Rorty, it means giving up on the idea of philosophy with a capital "P" (1982a). Each eschews the foundationalist aspiration of epistemology, particularly the idea the mind can be set over and against an autonomous metaphysical reality to which it has access through its *representations*. The consequence, Rorty contends, is that philosophy must give up its pretense to be "queen science," passing judgment on the merit of any and all knowledge claims in terms of its allegedly uniform and universal epistemological standards (1979).

Unlike Nietzschians, however, post-epistemologists deny that forsaking the quest for epistemological foundations requires forsaking normative judgment in the process and thereby limiting oneself to an exclusively *deconstructivist* activity. Rorty is content with "continuing the conversation" (1979, p. 394). He opts for the vocabulary of social hope he associates with Dewey over the vocabulary of power and oppression he associates with Foucault. While admitting that both vocabularies are ultimately "ungrounded," he contends that Dewey's vocabulary provides a more useful guide to social life and research (1982b).

Taylor shares much with Rorty, but his form of argument is closer to that customarily associated with epistemological investigation. That is, rather than resting his argument on an ungrounded choice between vocabularies, Taylor explicitly deploys reason to criticize the Nietzschian perspective.

Taylor agrees with the Nietzschians that the traditional foundationalist project of epistemology, the "epistemological construal," must be abandoned. And he also agrees that in doing so, "no construal [of knowledge] is quite innocent, something is always suppressed ... and some interlocutors are always disadvantaged relative to others ...." (1995b, p. 17). Still, there must be some "epistemic gain" that is realized by abandoning the epistemological construal. Taylor aligns himself with the "defenders of critical reason," whose project he describes as follows:

> For all its radical break with tradition, this kind of philosophy would in one respect be in continuity with it. It would be carrying further the demand for self-clarity about our nature as knowing agents, by adopting a better and more critically defensible notion of

what this entails. Instead of searching for an impossible foundational justification of knowledge ... we would now conceive this self-understanding as awareness about the limits and conditions of our knowing .... (1995b, p. 14)

A special version of post-epistemology is "naturalized epistemology." Like post-epistemological views in general, naturalized epistemology rejects the quest for epistemological foundations as fruitless (e.g., Goldman, 1995). It also denies a sharp dividing line between the descriptive and the normative. Naturalized epistemology differs from the versions of post-epistemology exemplified by thinkers such as Rorty and Taylor in being more programmatic. That is, it has retained to a large degree the traditional goal of epistemological investigation of explicating and improving the standards of knowledge and knowledge production. In its most general terms, naturalized epistemology is a pragmatic view, the project of which is to critique and improve scientific practices beginning with the practices themselves. Larry Laudan (1996), prominent among naturalized epistemologists, suggestively labels this project "normative naturalism. "

Controversies continue to rage over just what approach to epistemology is on the right track, and it is beyond my purposes in this chapter to defend any one position. My purpose is limited to getting clearer on what counts as an epistemology, an epistemological issue, and so forth, and on distinguishing among several alternatives on the current scene in order to permit getting clear on just what a biased epistemology might be. I now turn to that question.

What is a Biased Epistemology?

From among the synonyms for bias I listed earlier, concepts like "prejudiced," "partial," and "close-minded" apply better to bias in its epistemological sense than concepts like "self-serving," "unreasonable," and "unfair." This is so because epistemological bias is more deep-seated, subtle, and unconscious than the kind of bias that characterizes, say, partisan political wrangling. These features complicate the task of discerning whether an epistemology is biased, and so does the dialectical relationship that exists between the normative and descriptive elements of epistemology.

In the remainder of this section I try to find my way through what is a tangled thicket. I begin by examining the path suggested by James Scheurich and Michelle Young (1997), which, in my view, leads to a dead end. It is worth examining, however, because it explicitly addresses the issue of epistemological bias in educational research and because it caused quite a stir when it appeared in the *Educational Researcher*, the flagship journal of the American Educational Research Association. It also provides a good foil for the subsequent, more promising analyses of epistemological bias I consider.

Scheurich and Young maintain that virtually all of educational research is grounded in biased epistemology. They focus on "racist" epistemologies in particular, among which they include "positivisms, postpositivisms, neo-realisms, interpretivisms, constructivisms, the critical tradition, and postmod-ernisms/poststructuralisms" (p. 4). Now, this is a long and overlapping list for which Scheurich and Young provide very little in the way of specifics. It also excludes certain important contemporary epistemological views, such as pragmatism. But I'll not pursue those matters here. Instead, I focus on several broader issues.

Scheurich and Young claim that the epistemological views on their list are racist because they are outgrowths of "civilizational racism." That is, the white race has dominated the world for some time, and the premise of white suprem-acy on which this domination is based permeates Western epistemology. This kind of reasoning exemplifies what elementary logic books call the "genetic fallacy." Although Scheurich and Young's omnibus assessment of Western epi-stemology has some *prima facie* merit, it is woefully lacking in details. Certain epistemologies may indeed be racially biased. Explicating how and why this is so, however, requires considerably more detail than is provided by reference to the vague and amorphous notion of "civilizational racism." This is especially pressing in light of the fact that some of views, especially critical theory, have been formulated with an explicit focus on the identification and elimination of domination and oppression, racial and otherwise.

That the epistemologies-in-use of social and educational research have been and continue to be tinged with racial bias doesn't mean that epistemology—the *study* of the nature and justification of knowledge—must be uniformly guilty of the same charge. On the contrary, with the exception of thoroughgoing anti-epistemological views, epistemological investigation can provide the normative standpoint from which to criticize epistemologies-in-use. (As we shall see later, this is an important part of certain feminist approaches to epistemology.)

In a related vein, it is difficult to see how, given *their* epistemological view, Scheurich Young can make the charge of bias stick against other epistemological views. In particular, they exhibit a rather strong epistemological relativism, to the point where researchers choose from among epistemologies the one that "fits" with their "social history" (1997, p. 10). This makes it look like epi-stemological investigation is on a par with values-clarification: "I like being a pragmatist because that fits with my working class background, but you are free to be a Platonist if that fits with your aristocratic legacy." This is a significant mischaracterization of the nature of epistemological controversy. Those in-volved in such controversy stake out positions which they embrace as *generally more adequate than the alternatives*. This goes as much for postmodernists[3] feminists, and Afrocentrists as it does for positivists.

Furthermore this problem, Scheurich and Young include anti-epistemological views such as postmodernism among the menu of epi-stemologies. This papers over an important part of what is at stake on the current epistemological scene, for *having a position on epistemology* is no more interchangeable with *having an epistemology* than *having a position on astrology* is interchangeable with *having an astrology*. An anti-epistemological view, as the name suggests, takes a critical and dismissive position toward epistemology. On such a view, all claims to knowledge are equally biased or, depending on how one looks at it, equally incapable of bias. This follows by extension of the analysis provided in the first section. That is, just as "all claims are biased" renders the concept of bias vacuous, in general, "all epistemologies are biased" renders the concept of epistemological bias vacuous, in particular.

Finally, Scheurich and Young pass lightly, if not completely, over the distinction between epistemology and research methods. But a given study or a program of study can be criticized for being biased, outrageously so, without resort to epistemological principles. A community of researchers can agree on the nature and justification of knowledge and yet disagree about whether accepted research methods have been applied in an unbiased way. Consider the arguments provided in Stephen J. Gould's celebrated *Mismeasure of Man* (1981). Among the reasons that Gould gives for claiming that the history of research on intelligence is racially (as well as gender) biased is suppression of evidence (e.g., throwing out disconfirming results), ignoring relevant complexity (e.g., that women have smaller brains but also smaller bodies), employing bad measurement technique (e.g., using soft material that is subject to packing in measuring cranial size), employing questionable statistical analysis procedures (e.g., factor analysis in isolating IQ), among others. The important point to note is that Gould's criticisms do not require recourse to epistemology; they may be advanced *within* an epistemological perspective. (Indeed, the admonition not to suppress evidence or ignore relevant complexity applies to any epistemological perspective).

In sum, Scheurich and Young provide a dubious account of epistemological bias. At best, their view is too all encompassing and too lacking in specifics to be of much help in understanding the nature of epistemological bias and its source. At worst, it renders the notion of epistemological bias empty. But there are more promising analyses of epistemological bias. Below I consider several.

Positivism has been the primary target of charges of bias in social research. In his seminal "Interpretation and the Sciences of Man" (1987), Charles Taylor provides a general version of the critique. He argues that positivistic ("empiricist") epistemology of social science seeks to avoid interpretation—to "break out" of the "hermeneutical circle"—by grounding itself in "brute data" that require no interpretation. On Taylor's view, social life cannot be understood, or even accurately described, without "meanings" that humans pervasively interpret. In turn, such meanings can only be understood in terms of norms internal to social practices. By forcing social reality into a pre-interpreted framework of concepts, external to social practices, positivistic social science is biased—

prejudiced, closed-minded, and partial—in its account of social reality. And the problem is not confined to lack of detail and nuance. The threat of bias is fundamental, and becomes more and more problematic the farther removed the groups studied are from typical social norms and practices presupposed by the researcher. Taylor illustrates this point in terms of what is involved in applying the concept of "bargaining" across cultures.

> It is reported about the traditional Japanese village that the foundation of its social life was a powerful form of consensus, which puts a high premium on unanimous decision. ... [O]ur idea of bargaining, with the assumption of distinct autonomous parties in willed relationship, has no place there ... [W]hatever word of their language we translate as "bargaining," must have an entirely different gloss .... But this different gloss is *not just a difference of vocabulary, but also one of social reality* (1987, p. 53, emphasis added).

For Taylor, the only way to adequately understand social behavior is from the inside, in terms of its own meanings. And this leaves open the possibility of cases in which the only way you can gain an adequate understanding of a social group different from your own is to "change yourself" (1987, p. 77).

John Stanfield (1993) offers criticisms of positivistic social science that are consistent with Taylor's but that focus specifically on racial bias in American and European sociology. According to Stanfield, racial classifications employed in sociological research, e.g., Black and White, are reifications, born of race-centered societies. Framing research on race in terms of such categories ("brute data" categories for Taylor) homogenizes various groups, particularly the racially oppressed, and limits the identities available to their members to ascribed stereotypes. Such categories operate in conjunction with "evolutionary cognitive presumptions," according to Stanfield, where the dominant white culture is taken to be the standard of the most highly evolved, into which other cultural groups should be enculturated.

Stanfield's remedy for the kind of racial biases he describes is for researchers to pay much greater attention to the presuppositions relevant to race and values embedded in their general epistemologies-in-use, whether their research methods be quantitative, qualitative, or some combination. Researchers should also strive for participatory research that includes research subjects in determining what would improve the quality of their lives. Related to this, researchers should avoid the evolutionary cognitive perspective that presupposes there is a one best way of social life.

In addition to the attention it has received by thinkers such as Taylor and Stanfield, the issue of epistemological bias has also received considerable attention from feminist scholars (especially as it relates to the subjectivity/objectivity distinction). Of course, attempting to sketch a uniform feminist position would be wrong-headed, for the range of feminist views is broad and is marked by significant internal disagreement. I thus limit the discussion to a few central thinkers who employ feminist insights to correct the bias they perceive to be deeply embedded in "malestream" epistemology of social science.

Sandra Harding is a leading feminist philosopher, widely know for "standpoint epistemology." In her view, eliminating bias from social research requires more than merely requiring that researchers avoid "bad science" by better observing the canons of traditional (positivistic) social research so that sampling, the formulation of research questions, and so forth, are not overtly biased toward men. Although this would be an advance in her view, it leaves untouched a deeper kind of bias associated with the limited, predominately white male perspective on social arrangements and activities that, in turn, limits what can be perceived and conjectured. Contrary to the frequent criticism of positivistic research that it is overly objective, Harding turns the table, contending that "... it is not that [positivism] is too rigorous or too 'objectifying' ... it is *not rigorous* or objectifying *enough* ...." (1993, pp. 50–51).

"Strong objectivity," according to Harding, "requires that the subjects of knowledge be placed in the same critical, causal plane as the objects of knowledge" (1993, p. 69). This requires including a much broader range of researchers and participants than has been customary in social research and affording to hitherto marginalized groups a privileged epistemological position. Precisely because they have been frustrated by and marginalized from social processes, their perspective—or "standpoint"—enables them to better discern the workings of such processes and to ask the right questions about them. By contrast, the workings of social processes are taken for granted and therefore largely invisible to the mainstream. Deliberately including marginalized standpoints and empowering them with a significant voice is Harding's way of reducing bias in social research (or, in her terms, of moving from "weak" to "strong" objectivity) .

Thinkers such as Lorraine Code and Patricia Hill Collins have looked deeply into the epistemological role played by social position and history. Code (1993) focuses her attention on what she calls "S knows that p" epistemology, where "S" is the knower and "p" is the object of knowledge. Code objects to this formulaic approach on the grounds that it presupposes a conception of objectivity in which the characteristics of "S" and "p" are irrelevant.

In the case of "S," Code contends that the kinds of beliefs that various researchers bring to studies are in no way irrelevant to evaluating the warrant of their conclusions. The personal and theoretical value orientations of social researchers are under the influence of the broader socio-historical context, and at least partially determine what "facts" are thinkable and are likely to be found. (In this vein, Code would find it no coincidence that the *Bell Curve* was released when it was, into a political environment in which rationalizing racial inequality was relatively congenial to dominant interests.)

These value orientations are not (should not be) immune from critical scrutiny or papered over with the honorific "Science has proved ..." (p. 27). Positivistic social science dodges this kind of scrutiny by cloaking itself in its claimed objectivity and value-freedom. Echoing Harding, Code claims this stance reduces rather than enhances objectivity, for "objectivity *requires* taking subjectivity into account" (1993, p. 32). Echoing Stanfield, Code claims that because positivistic social science is fundamentally blind to its value orientations, "inquiry stops right where it should begin" (p. 30).

In the case of the "p" in the formula, Code distinguishes the objects of knowledge in social science from other objects of knowledge where the idea of a "brute fact" is more applicable, as in "It is a hot sunny day." Echoing Taylor, she contends that an interpretive epistemology is required in social science. The objects of knowledge in social science, the "p"s in the formula "S knows that p," possess subjectivities, just like the "S"s. Thus, they cannot be known in the "unsubtle way" that the objects of physics are known. The way other persons are known is a special way of knowing, but not thereby necessarily inferior. Indeed, Code suggests it is the most fundamental way of knowing. Turning the typical view of what counts as knowledge on its head, she quips:

> [I]t is certainly no more preposterous to argue that people should try to know physical objects in the nuanced way that they know their friends than it is to argue that they should try to know people in the unsubtle way they often claim to know physical objects. (p. 37)

Code suggests that the historical exclusion of women from academic communities has resulted in white men dominating these communities and not engaging in dialogue with anyone but themselves. A certain set of assumptions, practices, and "we saying" has evolved unchecked by members of other groups. According to Code, women should be included in order to problematize what has been left largely unexamined and to serve as "an experimental control ... so that every inquiry, assumption and discovery is analyzed for its place in and implications for the prevailing sex/gender system, in its intersections with the systems that sustain racism, homophobia, and ethnocentrism" (p. 31).

Patricia Hill Collins (1991) focuses specifically on the epistemological role of African American women in sociology. She thus helps flesh out standpoint epistemology in terms of a particularly illuminating case.

Collins characterizes the position of African American women in sociology as that of the "outsider within"—someone caught between the two worlds of academic sociology and African American womanhood. Because of her special predicament, she does not have her identity exclusively defined by either world but nonetheless has a good grasp of each. This position provides certain advantages in ascertaining social reality, according to Collins. In general, the outsider within is better able to detect the mismatch between the assumptions, predilections, and categories of social research and what her own experience tells her. Related to this, she is also better able to identify and problematize what is taken for granted by sociological insiders, for example, that the oppression of African American women is complexly "linked" to race, gender, and class, not just the sum of these sources of oppression.

Like Harding and Code, Collins believes that including and legitimating the perspective of the historically marginalized can advance social research. And Collins does not restrict outsider within status to African American women. White women, Black men, other people of color, working class persons, and religious minorities can all learn from the experience of Black women and contribute from their own perspectives.

The epistemological projects of Harding, Code, and Collins are *naturalized* in comparison to *foundationalist* epistemological projects, and are therefore closely tied to the fabric and practices of social life. Nonetheless, epistemological bias should be distinguished from forms of bias in social research that are less far-reaching and less fundamental. For example, feminists have by-and-large found qualitative research methods quite congenial to their aims, largely because such methods are potentially much more able to capture the diversity of perspectives or "voices" than quantitative methods are. However, the use of qualitative methods does not *per se* eliminate bias. As Cannon, Higgenbotham, and Leung (1991) argue, under-sampling of marginalized groups can be as much of a threat to qualitative methods as to quantitative ones. From the other direction, using quantitative methods does not *per se* engender bias either (Jayaratne & Stewart, 1991). Whether it does depends on the broader research framework in which these methods are embedded.

Conclusion: Controlling Bias Through Inclusion

Generally speaking, the thinkers discussed in the preceding section provide a normatively grounded epistemology that aspires to be free of bias and that incorporates principles and procedures that function to remove bias from epistemologies-in-use. The idea that inclusion, particularly of historically marginalized groups, provides better—less biased and more objective—social research is a prominent theme, especially among the feminists, Harding, Code, and Collins. (It is also a theme in Scheurich and Young (1997). Despite my reservations about the analysis in which they couch it, this is one place where I am in agreement with them.)

In the final section, I develop the idea of inclusion as a means of bias control more fully. But first I digress and briefly consider two other proposals for bias control in educational research: Alan Peshkin's (1988) and Lois Heshusius' (1994). These views are worth considering because of the alternative perspectives they provide from within the educational research community.

Peshkin (1988) urges educational researchers to move beyond merely acknowledging that their subjectivities "filter," "shape," "skew," "misconstrue"

(p. 17) what they are investigating: they should self-consciously reflect on the details of how their subjectivities manifest themselves throughout the research process. In this way, researchers' subjectivities may be "tamed," according to Peshkin, through a "formal, systematic monitoring of the self" (p. 20). Employing such a procedure, they can progress toward escaping the "thwarting biases that subjectivity engenders" (p. 21).

Heshusius (1994) sees a fundamental flaw in approaches to bias control such as the one recommended by Peshkin. According to her, attempting to spell out and observe "procedural subjectivity" amounts to bringing objectivity in through the backdoor. And "educational researchers," she asserts, "no longer see objectivity as a life option" (p. 15). Heshusius' alternative is a "participatory mode of consciousness" that "results from the ability to temporarily let go of all preoccupation with the self and move into a state of complete attention" (p. 17). She rejects the "possibility of a regulated distance between self and other" (p. 15) that she contends is presupposed by a view like Peshkin's.

Heshusius takes it as a given that objectivity is an untenable ideal. This is in stark contrast to the idea that objectivity is an ideal that should be retained but that must be re-conceptualized so as to take subjectivity into account. Heshusius' view is highly problematic for a number of reasons, many of which have already been discussed in this chapter and elsewhere in this book.[4] The new twist is her idea that the phenomenon of losing consciousness of oneself has deep epistemological and ontological implications and somehow enables getting around Peshkin's problem. It is very difficult to see how it does this, particularly in light of the fact that it simply reintroduces the problems that beset *Verstehen*, "going native," and the like.[5]

The problem with Peshkin's suggestion is that it is far too limited to effectively control bias. I have no objection to his admonition to educational researchers to pay close attention to their own biases, but this won't take them very far. A central tenet of the kind of "standpoint epistemology" described above is that educational researchers lack certain relevant social experience and knowledge because they are unavoidably socially and historically situated. Thus, they *can't* supply all of what is needed to control bias; what is needed can only by supplied by including a diversity of perspectives.

This leads back to idea of controlling bias through inclusion. Two kinds of bias control through inclusion may be distinguished: inclusion in research communities and inclusion in samples. I consider the latter first.

Inclusion in samples

Including a diversity of perspectives in social science samples is warranted on the straightforward methodological principle of unbiased sampling. In this *thin* sense of inclusion, sampling from a diversity of types of humans in social scientific research differs very little from sampling from a diversity of types of rocks in geological research. The situation in social science is typically more complicated, however, requiring a *thick* sense of inclusion.

By a thick sense of inclusion I mean a sense of inclusion that goes beyond the merely formal, a sense that, consistent with an overarching interpretive approach, taps the "voices" of research subjects (more about this in Chapter 9). This typically calls for qualitative research methods, particularly when the "insider's" voice is unknown or unclear and tapping it is thus the only route to an accurate understanding of social practices. Quantitative methods have other uses in overall studies, for example, to depict large patterns of income, levels of education, school achievement, and so forth. However, although quantitative methods do not necessarily distort voice, they must be used with considerable reflection and care. They are more prone to the kind of biases associated with pre-interpreted categories documented by Taylor (1987) and Stanfield (1991) than are qualitative methods.

Preventing people from expressing their views and thus from engaging in the democratic ideal of "conscious social reproduction" (Gutmann, 1987) is an injustice that good social research should avoid. Thus, thick inclusion is a moral requirement of social research. But this should not obscure the fact that it is also an epistemological requirement: thick inclusion engenders more objective, less biased results. That the epistemological and moral requirements of social research come together in this way around inclusion should be neither surprising nor problematic.[6]

Inclusion in the community of researchers

As Code (1993) observes, including hitherto excluded groups within research communities provides a form of "experimental control," a check on the biases of the homogeneous and insular groups that have historically made up such communities. But not everyone can perform the role; there are at least two qualifications that candidates for it must possess: (1) they must come from an appropriate group (e.g., one whose members can bring knowledge of a marginalized "standpoint") and (2) they must have the appropriate scholarly expertise (e.g., one that permits them to engage in debate and criticism rooted in an area of study).

The first requirement points out again how epistemological and moral requirements come together around inclusion. Inclusion of individuals from diverse standpoints in research communities functions epistemologically to reduce bias in the understanding of social life. Complementing and intertwined with this goal, it also functions morally to reduce power imbalances that result in domination and oppression. And this dovetailing of the epistemological and the moral is quite relevant to the means by which inclusion of individuals from diverse standpoints in research communities should be achieved. It provides especially strong support for the kind of *qualifications defense* of affirmative action provided by thinkers such as Gerald Dworkin (1977) and Amy Gutmann (1987), at least when applied to positions in social research. On this view, an African American man, for example, has a *prima facie qualification for advancing social research* that a white man can't have.

The second requirement, appropriate scholarly expertise, is an extension of the first, and is exceedingly nettlesome.[7] The fundamental problem is that if social research communities are, indeed, infected with significant bias, the accepted standards and beliefs surrounding judgments about expertise are infected as well. This leads to the following dilemma: those very individuals who should be included to correct bias either will be excluded for lack of scholarly expertise, or will be included because they have assimilated the status quo standards and beliefs. (Of course, a closely related dilemma confronts the evaluation of scholarly performance, after academic positions have been secured.)

It is very difficult to avoid getting skewered by on one or the other horn of this dilemma. Collins' idea of legitimating the "outsider within" provides one promising tack. In general, it should be clear that the effort to control epistemological bias—indeed, to control all forms of bias in educational research—requires paying attention not only to inclusiveness in the conduct of given research studies. It requires paying attention to the inclusiveness of the community of researchers as well.

Notes

1 "Epistemologies-in-use" is useful in the present context. It is the same idea, however, as Kaplan's (1964) "logics-in-use," which was pivotal in the argument for "compatibilism" in Chapter 3.

2 The complication here is that the positivists were enamored of science, and used their description—or "explication"—of it to critique claims of virtually all other modes of knowledge.

3 Of course, the postmodernist view, at least in its "strong" versions (Benhabib, 1995), is that epistemology should be thoroughly repudiated.

4 The arguments of Chapters 3 through 5 are each relevant, and especially 5. Heshusius takes the interpretive turn in the "postmodernist" direction that rejects objectivity, truth, rationality, etc., wholesale. At the same time, she wants to preserve some place for moral critique, which her overall view undermines.

5 The idea of "compatibilism" that I defended in Chapter 3 is of particular relevance here. The brand of anti-positivism associated with "incompatibility thesis" that defines itself in polar opposition to positivism and that calls for a completely different kind of social scientific understanding confined to empathizing with "insiders" has serious problems of its own.

6 But see Siegel (1996) and my critique (1998).

7 Once again, see Siegel (1996) and Howe (1998).

III

ETHICAL AND POLITICAL FRAMEWORKS

Chapter 8

THE INTERPRETIVE TURN AND RESEARCH ETHICS

The ethics of social and educational research has been significantly complicated over the last several decades as a consequence of the interpretive turn and the ever increasing use of qualitative research methods that has accompanied it. In this chapter, I refer to the ways research ethics has been framed before and after the interpretive turn as the *traditional* and *contemporary* problematics, respectively. The distinction is a heuristic one. I do not mean to suggest that the interpretive turn occurred at any very precise point in time or that it has completely won out.

Embedded in the distinction between the traditional and contemporary problematics is another, between the protection of research participants ("research subjects" in the traditional vocabulary) and research misconduct. I will focus on the former, because it is with respect to the relationship between researchers and research participants that the interpretive turn poses its greatest challenges. Issues that customarily come under the heading of research misconduct, such as data fabrication, plagiarism, the exploitation of graduate students, and so forth, have been less affected.

The Traditional Problematic

The traditional problematic rests on a rather sharp line between the "prescriptive" (moral-political) component of social research and the "descriptive" (scientific-methodological) component (Beauchamp, Faden, Wallace, & Walters, 1982). It divides questions concerning the morals and politics of social scientific studies from questions concerning their scientific merits, and pursues them relatively independently. Indeed, not keeping these domains separated is often considered the mark of biased social research or of political advocacy under the name of research.

In my discussion of the traditional problematic, I follow suit and separate the ethics of social research from broader political and methodological issues. I save raising questions about this maneuver for my discussion of the "contemporary problematic."

Protecting individual autonomy has long been a central principle in Western moral-political thought. That it should also occupy a central place in Western thought about the ethics of social research should thus come as no surprise.

The traditional controversy about autonomy has been cast in terms of Kantian versus utilitarian ethical frameworks. The Kantian (also non-consequentialist or deontological) framework employs "categorical" ethical principles, the most general of which is: *always treat persons as ends in themselves and never solely as means.* In this framework individual autonomy is fundamental, for respecting autonomy is tantamount to treating individuals as ends in themselves. By contrast, the utilitarian (also consequentialist or teleological) framework employs "hypothetical" ethical principles that are subsidiary to the uniform goal of maximizing the balance of benefits over harms. Thus, "always treat persons as ends" is binding only insofar as it also maximizes benefits. In this framework autonomy is instrumental.

Utilitarian reasoning is widely criticized for sanctioning unacceptable moral conclusions, in both theory and practice. In theory, one can imagine a society in which benefit is defined as what gives people pleasure and that fights to the death among enslaved combatants serve to maximize the total balance of pleasure over pain—a society in which by summing the pleasure experienced by the spectators and subtracting the pain experienced by the combatants, the total value would be higher than if the practice were prohibited. In practice, certain biomedical research (e.g., the Tuskegee study of the progression of untreated syphilis in African American men) as well as social research (e.g., Milgram's studies of obedience) receive their sanction from utilitarian reasoning when they are defended on the grounds that the harm done to research participants in the short term is outweighed by long term benefit of the knowledge produced.

To be sure, these are research practices that many (perhaps all) utilitarian theorists would condemn. Arguably, however, it is only by adopting *rule-utilitarianism* and providing utilitarian reasons for following moral rules independent of the calculation of specific benefit-harm ratios—only by providing utilitarian reasons for eschewing utilitarian reasoning in specific cases—that the unacceptable moral conclusions that follow from a thoroughgoing application of utilitarian reasoning can be blocked. Venturing deeply enough into moral philosophy to fully develop this point would take me too far afield from the task at hand. I thus adopt the more modest strategy of examining the most outstanding difficulty for utilitarianism in the context of research involving human participants and then showing how, whatever the ultimate theoretical foundations might be, the principles employed to govern the treatment of research participants are *de facto* Kantian.

The most outstanding difficulty for utilitarianism is specifying the benefits and harms that are to go into its calculations. Not only are people likely to disagree about what these are. An important corollary is that all morally relevant considerations must be cast in terms of benefits and harms, in which, for instance, the harms done to slaves who must fight to the death are put on the same scale as the benefits that accrue to those who enjoy watching such a spectacle. Otherwise, utilitarian calculations would not be possible.

MacIntyre contends that confinement to utilitarian benefits-harms calculations eliminates two kinds of morally relevant considerations in the context of social research: "wrongs" and "moral harms" (1982). Consider the famous Tearoom Trade study. Keeping his identity as a researcher secret, Laud Humphreys assumed the role of a lookout, a "watchqueen," in public restrooms as men engaged in homosexual acts. Arguably, the balance of benefits over harms in this study was positive; if not for the men actually involved in the study, then for gay men overall. (There has been much actual discussion along these lines, and Humphreys saw himself as producing overall beneficial effects by reducing homophobic stereotyping. See, for example, Beauchamp et al., 1982.) But restricting the relevant considerations to benefits and harms circumscribes the analysis in a way that excludes the question of whether deceiving these men did them a moral wrong, independent of the calculation of overall harms and benefits. It may be argued that Humphreys' deception of these men disregarded their dignity, their agency, and, in general, treated them as mere means for achieving other persons' ends. The response that treating persons as mere means is just one kind of harm to be entered into the benefit-harm calculation misses the point of the objection and begs the question in favor of utilitarianism's premise that all morally relevant considerations can be put on the same scale.

The Tearoom Trade example may also be used to illustrate the concept of "moral harms," the other morally relevant consideration eliminated by confinement to utilitarian benefit-harms calculations. According to MacIntyre, "Moral harm is inflicted on someone when some course of action produces in that person a greater propensity to commit wrongs" (1982, p. 178). It is a plausible conjecture that, as a result of Humphreys' study, the men in it were made more cynical and distrustful, and more inclined to treat others as mere means to pursuing their own ends. (The Tuskegee study provides a more dramatic example and one for which "moral harms" have been documented, e.g., Haworth, 1997.)

If inflicting moral harms is something that social research ought to avoid, then the justification for doing so has to be sought beyond utilitarian benefits-harms calculations. Moral harms cannot be routinely plugged into utilitarian benefit-harm calculations; rather, avoiding them places a fundamental constraint on the use to which such calculations can be put. This goes for moral wrongs as well because they involve the rights to self-determination and privacy—rights that in Dworkin's (1978) suggestive phraseology, "trump" utilitarian calculations.

As mentioned above, there is a version of utilitarianism that putatively avoids the kinds of criticisms just advanced, namely, rule-utilitarianism. Kelman (1982), a self-described rule-utilitarian, provides a good example of such a view applied specifically to the ethics of social research.

The benefit that Kelman ultimately seeks to maximize is the "fulfillment of human potentialities" (1982, p. 41). He concedes, however, the extreme difficulty involved in determining whether this applies in specific circumstances and, for this reason, rejects *act-utilitarianism*. He goes on to use "consistency with human dignity" as his criterion for moral evaluation (1982, p. 42), which he subsequently identifies (in language almost straight from Kant) with treating "individuals as ends in themselves, rather than as means to some extraneous ends" (1982, p. 43). In a related vein, under the rubric of "wider social values" (1982, p. 46), Kelman embraces the idea that social research should avoid engendering "diffuse harm," the "reduction of private space," and the "erosion of trust."

The parallel between Kelman's and MacIntyre's views on these points is striking. Corresponding to MacIntyre's admonition to avoid "moral wrongs," we have Kelman's admonition to treat persons as "ends in themselves;" corresponding to MacIntyre's admonition to avoid "moral harms," we have Kelman's to avoid "diffuse harms." In both cases, confinement to utilitarian benefit-harm calculations is viewed as morally inadequate. If moral justification is to be ultimately utilitarian, to ultimately fall under the rule of benefit-harm calculations, then it is not only individually defined benefits and harms that must be taken into account, but also benefits or harms to the moral health of individuals and of the human community overall.

This should explain why I would say that thinking about the ethical treatment of participants in social research is *de facto* Kantian. There is rather widespread agreement that whatever the ultimate justification for moral conclusions regarding the treatment of research participants might be, certain ethical principles should constrain the manner in which researchers may treat research participants in meeting the traditional utilitarian goals of advancing knowledge and otherwise benefiting society.

Informed consent is the most central of such ethical principles, and it is prominent in federal regulations governing social research. The basic idea is that it is up to research participants to weigh the risks and benefits associated with participating in a research project and up to them to then decide whether to participate. And they can only do this if they are informed about and understand what their participation in the research involves. In this way their autonomy is protected in a way it was not in the Tuskegee, Tearoom Trade, and Milgram studies. Informed consent is *de facto* Kantian because refusal to participate on the part of research participants is binding, even if their refusal results in failing to maximize presumed benefits.

Privacy is the second central principle in the traditional conception of the ethical treatment of social research participants, in addition to autonomy. Two subsidiary principles for protecting it are anonymity (not gathering identity specific data) and confidentiality (not revealing identity-specific data). The relationships among autonomy and informed consent, on the one hand, and privacy, confidentiality, and anonymity, on the other, are varied and complex.

In one view privacy is a kind of autonomy. For example, in the celebrated *Roe v. Wade* decision (1973) and the precedent on which it depended, *Griswold v. Connecticut* (1964), the right to privacy was invoked as equivalent to protecting the autonomy of individuals regarding abortion and birth control, respectively. In a related way, autonomy has also been advanced as the justification for protecting the privacy of medical records, school records, and social research data, on the grounds that the release of such information can restrict the options available to those about whom it is released. For example, depending on the circumstances, the release of medical records could reduce a person's employment opportunities, the release of school records could label a child and thereby restrict his or her life options, and the release of social science data could cause someone to be deported.

In a second view, privacy has an intrinsic value, tied to human dignity and security, and distinct from its relationship to autonomy. According to Arthur Caplan, "Privacy is a basic human need. Without privacy, it is not possible to develop or maintain a sense of self or personhood." Thus, the attempt to derive the right to privacy from the right to autonomy puts "the cart before the proverbial horse," he says (1982, p. 320). Save the limiting case of not choosing to be observed, the value of privacy may have little or no connection to self-determination. It is the value of having "private space" (e.g., Kelman, 1992), of being free from surveillance, from looking over one's shoulder, from humiliation and embarrassment, and the like, that privacy protects. Consider the reason one would not want to be observed by strangers going to the toilet or engaging in sex.

As it turns out, the requirement of informed consent diminishes the importance of determining which analysis of privacy is the correct one, and in which contexts. For part of the informed consent process is describing to participants just what the risks to their privacy might be, and what measures will be taken to insure anonymity or confidentiality. In this way, how important privacy might be, and why, largely devolves to individuals' exercise of autonomy.

The Contemporary Problematic

The traditional problematic is rooted in experimental and quasi-experimental, so-called "quantitative," research methodology, still the gold standard in medical research and the methodology traditionally predominant in the social sciences and education. Thus, the burgeoning of so-called "qualitative" research methodologies over the past several decades poses a potential challenge to the adequacy of the traditional approach. To be sure, the challenge is not new—field researchers have long contended with it—but it is more prominent, pressing, and pervasive than it once was. The advent of federal regulations is one stimulus. New and revitalized perspectives in moral theory that question the centrality of autonomy—communitarianism, care theory, and postmodernism, for instance—is another.

The interpretive turn in social research is implicated in both of these developments. Given the interpretivist perspective, beliefs, attitudes, customs, and identities—virtually everything that makes humans what they are—are created and exist only within social relationships, relationships in which language use looms large. No neutral scientific language, à la positivism, exists with which to describe social life wholly from the outside, as it were. Social life is "dialogical," as Charles Taylor (1994) puts it, and thus the methodology of social research must be so as well: it must seek out and listen carefully to "voices" embedded in their social context to gain a true understanding of what people are saying and why they do what they do. And dialogue itself has consequences: beliefs, culture norms, and the like, are not just there, waiting to be uncovered, but are negotiated and "constructed" via the interactions among researchers and those they study.

The implications of this methodological-cum-epistemological shift in social research ethics may be divided into two general areas: *philosophical perspectives* and *procedural principles*. The former refers to the broad moral-political frameworks that underpin social and educational research; the latter, to the more specific principles employed to govern and evaluate social and educational research *vis-à-vis* ethics.

Philosophical Perspectives

The interpretive perspective jettisons the positivistic fact/value dichotomy and, along with it, the idea that social and educational researchers can confine themselves to neutral descriptions and effective *means* toward "technical control" (Fay, 1975). Rather, value-laden descriptions and *ends* are always pertinent and always intertwined with means. Because each is part-and-parcel of social science research, the researcher has no way to avoid moral-political commitments by placing ethics and politics in one compartment and scientific merit in another. As MacIntyre says,

> The social sciences are moral sciences. That is, not only do social scientists explore a human universe centrally constituted by a variety of obediences to and breaches of, conformities to and rebellions against, a host of rules, taboos, ideals, and beliefs about goods, virtues, and vices ... *their own explorations of that universe are no different in this respect from any other form of human activity* (1982, p. 175, emphasis added).

This general stance is one that the contemporary perspectives of communitarianism, care theory, postmodernism, critical theory, and contemporary liberalism converge on.[1]

Communitarianism

Communitarianism locates morality within a given community and its shared norms and "practices" (MacIntyre, 1981). Accordingly, what is conceived as the morally good life has to be known from the inside and varies from one community to another. Because social and educational research cuts across communities that may differ from the social researcher's own, ensuring the ethical treatment of research participants who are members of such communities is doubly problematic. Not only is the traditional problem involved in protecting autonomy potentially complicated by difficulties in communication; the members of the communities they investigate may not share a commitment to the fundamental values that guide social and educational researchers.

For example, certain communities do not place a high value on individual autonomy (the Amish perhaps being the most well known case). As such, it is not up to individual community members to give their informed consent to have social researchers peering in to the social life of the community, for it is not always *theirs* to give. The community may reject the way of explaining and rendering community life transparent associated with social science, and may not want its practices understood and portrayed in these terms. True, an individual community member who agreed to participate in developing such a portrayal might be viewed as a rogue who was wronging the community, but the social researcher could not avoid the charge that it was he or she who was the true instigator of such an "act of aggression" (MacIntyre, 1982, p. 179). The social researcher has no wholly neutral position from which to conduct research. "The danger" in believing otherwise, MacIntyre says, "is that what is taken to be culturally neutral by the [social researcher] may be merely what his or her own culture takes to be culturally neutral" (1982, pp. 183-184).

The ethical predicament for social and educational researchers raised here is close to the one historically raised under the anthropological concept of "cultural relativism." The difference is that it may now be recognized as a pervasive problem that applies to the broad range of "qualitative" social and educational research conducted across a broad range of cultural contexts and groups, not only to exotic ones.

Care theory

Care theory is a close cousin of communitarianism. Both emphasize concrete circumstances and the specific demands on individuals associated with the "view from here" over ideal circumstances and the demands placed on individuals by abstract principles associated with "the view from nowhere" (Nagel, 1986). On the other hand, care theory embraces if not a culturally neutral ideal, one that nonetheless is to be applied across cultural encounters. According to Nel Noddings (1984), caring is the ethical universal.

Noddings (1986) applies the ethics of care specifically to educational research. Her first thesis is that the relationship between researchers and participants ought to exemplify caring, particularly trust and mutual respect; her second thesis broadens the first so as to apply to the educational research enterprise as a whole. According to Noddings, the choice of research questions and the overall conduct of the research ought to be based on their potential to contribute to caring school communities. Educational research shouldn't be conducted on the basis of mere intellectual curiosity, much less should it be conducted in a way that is likely to be harmful to individual students or groups of students, or destructive of school communities. Educational research should be *"for* teaching," Noddings says, not simply *"on* teaching" (1986, p. 506). Ignoring these concerns renders the traditional emphasis on autonomy and privacy incomplete, at best.

Postmodernism

Postmodernism shares the premise found in communitarianism and care theory that social and educational research cannot first, isolate the descriptive component of social research from its moral component and second, insure the ethical treatment of research participants by obtaining their informed consent and protecting their autonomy and privacy. But the postmodernist critique is more radical. Whereas communitarianism and care theory identify dangers with and lacunas in the traditional conception, postmodernism questions the very existence of the integral selves upon which the traditional conception is based.

On the postmodern analysis, individuals are not capable of freely directing their own lives, but are always enmeshed in and shaped by relationships of knowledge/power. These "regimes of truth," as Foucault calls them, serve to "normalize" individual selves and render them acquiescent and "useful" *vis-à-vis* the institutions of modern society (Foucault, 1970). Traditional forms of social and educational research foist such regimes of truth on participants, however masked the nature of their activity might be. When practiced unreflectively, these forms of research create a situation in which far from fostering autonomy, or even respecting it, social and educational researchers are accomplices in social domination.

Given a "strong" version of this thesis (Benhabib, 1995), postmodernism can provide little or no guidance about what direction social and educational research should take to avoid domination.[2] For if there are no criteria of truth, justice, and reason independent of the perspective of a given regime of truth and the position of power researchers occupy within it, then there are no criteria for distinguishing *abuses* of power from its (unavoidable) *uses*.

In educational research, postmodernism typically takes a less extreme form. As Stronach and MacLure put it, a "positive reading" is required (1997). The basic idea is that researchers must be alert to the often subtle, asymmetrical relationships of power that threaten to oppress participants. Accordingly, participants must take a much more active role than they have traditionally in shaping the research process, and in challenging its methods and findings as it unfolds. In general, educational researchers should be much more suspicious than they typically are of the idea that educational research is *per se* a progressive force. Not unrelated to this, the validity of the findings of educational research cannot be divorced from how it treats relationships of power (e.g., Lather, 1991b; 1994).

Critical theory

The *sine qua non* of critical theory is its characterization of and opposition to "technical control" as the primary or only role for social and educational research (e.g., Fay, 1975). Technical control is closely associated with positivist social research; it is the goal educational research adopts when it proceeds by bracketing moral and political ends and investigating only the means of achieving them. The current testing/accountability movement launched by a *Nation at Risk* (National Commission on Excellence in Education, 1983) is illustrative. First, the end, economic competitiveness, is bracketed and left to politicians and policymakers. Second, coming up with effective means in the form of testing/accountability regimens is left to the expert researchers. Finally, research sanctioned testing regimens are then put in place with little or no input from those most affected—teachers, students, and parents.

The means/ends bifurcation is open to at least three criticisms. First, means are relative to ends. Adopting the end of economic competitiveness *ipso facto* restricts the range of relevant means to those associated with achieving it. Accordingly, such means are laden with the end of promoting economic competitiveness. Furthermore, whether something is a means or an end typically depends on its place in a longer chain of means and ends. For example, achievement in math and science is an end relative to instruction but a means relative to economic competitiveness.

Second, means themselves are subject to value constraints, even relative to some end. If it could be shown that an effective means for improving economic competitiveness is putting all "at risk" students in forced labor camps, I trust that no one would seriously entertain such a policy. Unfortunately, the general point this example illustrates often gets lost when dealing with less obvious examples of morally questionable means—talent tracking, for instance.

Third, and most fundamentally, positivist technical control is irremediably undemocratic. Presupposing the ends of those with the power to formulate them, and then employing expert researchers to investigate the means to effect such ends engenders technocracy rather than democracy. Genuine democracy requires that participation be respected as an end in itself. Social and educational research in service of democracy requires that no end or ends should be settled on ahead of time, prior to and independent of the investigation of means. Rather dialogue about both should be free, open, inclusive and "undistorted" by imbalances of power. From the perspective of critical theory, a fundamental role of social research is (should be) emancipation.

Contemporary liberal theory

Liberalism, particularly its utilitarian strand, has often been the target of the four perspectives just described. Utilitarianism generalizes a certain conception of individual rationality—maximize benefits over harms—to the level of ethics and social policy—maximize benefits over harms in the aggregate (e.g., Rawls, 1971). It is vulnerable at both levels. First, the view of rationality presupposed is not shared across groups and, worse, is not a particularly desirable one in any case. Second, extending the principle of utility maximization to the level of ethics and policy can result in wronging people in the way previously described by MacIntyre (1982). Finally, in the practice of social and educational research, the principle of utility maximization tends to work in tandem with the goal of technical control.

Utilitarianism was the major strand of liberalism until the appearance of John Rawls' *A Theory of Justice* in 1971, which has since been the point of departure for liberal thinking. The kind of "liberal-egalitarian" view (e.g., Kymlicka, 1990) that Rawls formulated constrains the principle of maximizing utility in the name of justice. Not only aggregate utility is morally relevant; utility (benefits) must be distributed so as to tend toward equality.

Two major criticisms of Rawls' theory are that it (1) presupposes a certain Western (and male) conception of rationality (maximize utility within constraints) and (2) conceives of policy making on the model of technical control (merely operating with a different distributive principle than utilitarianism). These come together in Iris Marion Young's (1990c) criticism of liberal-egalitarianism's commitment to what she calls the "distributivist paradigm." Liberal-egalitarianism identifies the disadvantaged who need to be compensated as part of its distributive (or re-distributive) scheme. Compensation takes the form of various social welfare programs, including educational ones. Insofar as those targeted for compensation are excluded from participating in the formulation such programs, what counts as being to their benefit is decided for them. They are thus rendered subject to the decision-making of the agents of technical control.

Contemporary liberal-egalitarians have taken this criticism seriously, and have proffered remedies aimed at preserving the viability of liberalism. The general strategy is to tilt liberalism's emphasis on equality away from the distribution of predetermined goods and toward participation in determining what those goods should be. As Kymlicka says,

> [I]t only makes sense to invite people to participate in politics (or for people to accept that invitation) if they are treated as equals ... And that is incompatible with defining people in terms of roles they did not shape or endorse (1991, p. 89).

The "participatory paradigm" (Howe, 1995) exemplified in Kymlicka's admonition is much more attuned to the interpretive turn in social and educational research than the distributivist paradigm. It fits with a model of research in which justice and equality are sought not only in the distribution of predetermined goods, but also in the status and voice of research participants.

Shared philosophical themes

The five perspectives have been portrayed in the most general terms. They, no doubt, differ in further, possibly irreconcilable, ways. Still, there are several shared themes across them that make for common ground with respect to the contemporary problematic.

First, as I indicated before, there is a strong tendency in what I have been calling the traditional problematic to distinguish the descriptive (scientific-methodological) component of social research from the prescriptive (moral-political) component. Each of the five alternative perspectives denies that social and educational research can be (ought to be) divided up in this way. On the contrary, social and educational research is (ought to be) framed by self-consciously chosen moral-political ends, for example, fostering caring communities or fostering equality and justice. It is thus no criticism of a given study that it adopts *some* moral-political perspective. Criticism arises instead with respect to just what that moral-political perspective is, as well as the consequences of framing research in terms of it.

Educational researchers might, and many no doubt do, ostensibly conduct research *on* teaching rather than *for* teaching, to use Noddings' (1986) distinction once again. But rather than getting rid of the question of what research might be *for*, they are merely closing their eyes to it. Any research that is used at all is used *for* something, and the range of uses is limited from the outset by how the research is conceived and designed. This casts a different light on research like Murray and Herrnstein's (1994) *The Bell Curve*. The problem is not that they engaged in research laden with moral-political values *per se*. The problem is that they denied this, and claimed to be simply following science where it led.

Second, social and educational research ought to have points of contact with the insiders' perspectives, with their "voices." In this way, the moral-political aims of social and educational research affect its methodology. Interpretive, or "qualitative," methods are best suited for getting at what these voices have to say.

Finally, each of the five perspectives militates against the race, gender, and class bias that have historically plagued social and educational research—forms of bias that grow out of the premise that the attitudes, beliefs, and reasoning of mainstream white males comprise the standard against which all other social groups must be measured (Stanfield, 1993).

Procedural Principles

The distinction between research ethics in the sense of procedural principles, and in the broader, philosophical sense is not hard-and-fast. For what questions are worth asking and how researchers are to conduct themselves in the process of answering them cannot be divorced from the overarching aims that research seeks to achieve. Nonetheless, there exists a *looseness of fit* between procedural principles and competing philosophical perspectives, such that reasonable agreement on what constitutes ethical conduct is (or should be) possible in the face of broader theoretical disagreements. Bearing in mind, then, that broader ethical obligations associated with broader moral-political perspectives are always lurking in the background, there remain general ethical implications of the interpretive turn in educational research that may be best understood in terms of special challenges posed by nuts and bolts of research methods.

Informed consent

Qualitative methods possess two features that quantitative methods lack (at least lack to a significant degree): *intimacy* and *open-endedness* (Howe & Dougherty, 1993; see also Wax, 1982, for a similar analysis). The features of intimacy and open-endedness significantly complicate protecting participants' autonomy and privacy, and complicate the researcher's moral life as well.

Qualitative methods are intimate insofar as they reduce the distance between researchers and participants in the conduct of social and educational research. Indeed, the growing preference for the term "participants"—who take an active role in "constructing social meanings"—over "subjects"—who passively receive "treatments"—testifies to the changed conception of relationships among human beings engaged in social and educational research that has attended the growth of qualitative methods. The face-to-face interactions associated with the techniques of interviewing and participant observation are in stark contrast to the kind of interactions required to prepare subjects for a treatment.

Qualitative methods are open-ended insofar as the questions and persons to which interviewing and participant observation may lead can only be roughly determined at the outset. This, too, is in stark contrast to the relatively circumscribed arena of questions and participants that characterizes quantitative methods.

What intimacy and open-endedness mean for researchers employing qualitative methods is that they are (whether they want or intend to or not) likely to discover secrets and lies as well as oppressive relationships. These discoveries may put research participants at risk in ways that they had not consented to and that the researcher had not anticipated. These discoveries may also put researchers in the position of having to decide whether they have an ethical responsibility to maintain the confidentiality of participants or to expose them, as well as having to decide whether to intervene in some way in oppressive relationships (see, e.g., Dennis, 1993; Roman, 1993).

Researchers employing quantitative methods can face the same problems. For instance, information can simply fall into their laps in the process of explaining a protocol and recruiting participants; a treatment may prove so obviously effective (or harmful) that the trial should be stopped; and so forth. Still, the odds of facing unforeseen ethical problems are surely much higher for researchers employing qualitative methods. Generally speaking, then, qualitative methods are more ethically uncertain and hazardous than quantitative methods.

Some researchers employing qualitative methods have recoiled at this suggestion, on the grounds that the current ways of thinking about and monitoring the ethics of social research are rooted in quantitative methods and are therefore inappropriate for qualitative methods (e.g., Lincoln, 1990; Murphy & Johannsen, 1990; Wax, 1982). Wax, who exemplifies this view, contends that informed consent "is both too much and too little" (1982, p. 44) to require of researchers employing qualitative methods ("fieldwork," to be precise). He says,

> [I]nformed consent is too much . . . in requesting formal and explicit consent to observe that which is intended to be observed and appreciated. Formal and explicit consent also appears overscrupulous and disruptive in the case of many of the casual conversations that are intrinsic to good fieldwork, where respondents (informants) are equal partners to interchange, under no duress to participate, and free either to express themselves or to withdraw into silence. On the other hand, informed consent is too little because fieldworkers so often require much more than consent; they need active assistance from their hosts, including a level of research cooperation that frequently amounts to colleagueship. (1982, p. 44)

Wax seems to go in two incompatible directions. When he claims that informed consent requires too much, he focuses on how it can be a nuisance and obstruct social research. He goes so far as to defend deceptive ("covert") research—research that suspends the requirement of informed consent—on explicitly utilitarian grounds: "... on a utilitarian basis, we can contend the wrongs incurred by the practice of covert fieldwork may be far outweighed by the social benefit ... " (p. 41). That it might be more difficult and more of a nuisance to obtain informed consent where qualitative methods are employed provides no principled reason for not doing so. It is hard to see Wax's argument as anything other than special pleading on behalf of qualitative methods. Researchers employing quantitative methods can offer the same kind of utilitarian arguments for deception.

When Wax claims that informed consent requires too little, he is, indeed, getting at something that distinguishes qualitative from quantitative methods. The mechanism of informed consent grew out of the kind of imbalance of power associated with the experimentalist tradition in which the researchers versus subjects distinction implies "subjection" on the part of the latter. "Informed consent," Wax says,

> is a troublesome misconstrual of ... field relationships because the field process is progressive and relationships are continually being negotiated, so that, if the research is going well, the fieldworker is admitted to successively deeper levels of responsibility together with being required to share communal intimacies ... (1982, p. 45)

According to Wax, the relationship between researchers and participants should exemplify "parity" and "reciprocity," and "where there is parity and reciprocity, the ethical quality of the relationship has progressed far beyond the requirements of 'informed consent'" (1982, p. 46).

This analysis is correct as far as it goes: the intimacy and open-endedness of qualitative methods distinguish them from quantitative methods and render informed consent more problematic. But it doesn't follow from this that the requirement of informed consent ought to be jettisoned where qualitative methods make it more difficult to obtain.

Wax construes informed consent as a one-shot, all-or-none event, the model that fits biomedical and experimentalist social research. But this is not the only form it might take. The underlying rationale for informed consent, after all, is the protection of autonomy and, in the way described previously, privacy. The one-shot approach to informed consent fails to provide these protections in light of the special features of qualitative research, namely, it's intimacy and open-endedness. But informed consent may be reconceived so that it better takes these features into account. In this vein, qualitative researchers themselves have proposed construing informed consent on the model of an ongoing "dialogue" (e.g., Smith, 1990) and have suggested periodic re-affirmations of consent (e.g., Cornett & Chase, 1989) as the procedural embodiment of this notion.

Yvonna Lincoln (1990) provides a more radical and far-reaching critique of the traditional emphasis on the protection of autonomy and privacy than the kind provided by Wax. Central to Lincoln's view is the fundamental gap she perceives between the logical- and post-positivistic "epistemologies" that allegedly underpin the traditional regulations and the phenomenological/constructivist "philosophies" she advocates. One of the more dubious of Lincoln's conclusions is that informed consent is less, not more, ethically hazardous in the case of research employing qualitative methods. Because its aim is to portray the "multiple social constructions that individuals hold," anything short of complete openness on the part of researchers doesn't even make sense for well executed "phenomenological and constructivist" research. As Lincoln sees things, it makes sense only for positivist-oriented researchers, who seek to converge on a " 'real' reality 'out there'" independent of individuals' constructions (1990, p. 280).

Lincoln takes a similarly dismissive stance toward the principle of privacy. The following summary points capture the substance as well as the tone of her position:

> First, privacy, confidentiality, and anonymity regulations were written under assumptions ["logical positivism and postpositivism"] that are ill suited to qualitative and/or phenomenological, constructivist philosophies; second, from some small preliminary studies, we now understand that respondents may be willing to give up strict privacy and anonymity rights for the larger right to act with agency in participating in the research efforts as full, cooperating agents in their own destinies; third, we . . . must trade the role of detached observer for that of professional participant. But, clearly, the issue is far more complex than simply fretting about privacy, anonymity, and confidentiality. (1990, p. 280)

The general view Lincoln advances is that the traditional emphasis on autonomy and privacy is grounded in positivism. But positivism is *"inadequate* and, indeed, *misleading* for human inquiry" (1990, p. 279), according to her. Because qualitative/phenomenological/constructivist researchers have repudiated positivism's quest for reality in favor of a quest for the meanings individuals construct, they seek to grant "coequal power" (1990, p. 279) to participants and have no reason to ever be anything but fully forthcoming with them.

Lincoln's analysis is more than a little problematic. Consider her second point above: ". . . respondents may be willing to give up strict privacy and anonymity rights for the larger right to act with agency in participating in the research efforts . . . " Well, they *may* be, but apparently it is they who should decide. And they decide, give their informed consent, under the conditions of uncertainty associated with the open-ended nature of qualitative methods. Nothing Lincoln says removes this uncertainty or the ethical hazard it creates.

More generally, Lincoln's view is remarkably oblivious to the kinds of ethical quandaries in which researchers employing qualitative methods can find themselves. Take the issue of researchers being less than forthcoming, or even deceptive, with participants. In fact, many sites of social research, including schools, do not exemplify equality among actors. Being open can serve to reinforce such inequality where those in power move to protect their positions. As I observed before, researchers employing qualitative methods can discover oppressive relationships they had not anticipated at the outset, for example, an abusive teacher, a racially based tracking scheme, a sexist curriculum. What to do about these discoveries is often arguable, and often depends on the particulars. But this much is clear: researchers cannot automatically get off the hook by distancing themselves from positivism and pushing on with the construction of meanings. As Dennis remarks regarding his use of participant observation to study race, it is sometimes necessary to "choose sides:"

> [F]ieldwork is often fraught with informational and emotional land mines between which and around which the researcher must maneuver . . . when issues involve racial justice, for instance, there is no question but that the researcher should be on the side of the excluded and oppressed. (1993, pp. 68–69)

Short of having to "choose sides," researchers employing qualitative methods are constantly faced with less dramatic reasons for refraining from being fully forthcoming with research participants. For example, in order to gain access to the voices of older Chicana women, Elisa Facio explains how she had to initially play up her role as a volunteer in the seniors' center that was the site of her research. That she was a student and, furthermore, was doing research, was revealed only later in the course of her research. Facio believed that the culture and social histories of these women required this kind of procedure, and citing Punch (1986), observed that participant observation "always involves impression management," including "alleviating suspicion." Nonetheless, she confessed to feeling "uncomfortable with the deceit and dissembling," as she put it, that "are part of the research role" (1993, p. 85).

Was Facio's incremental approach to consent ethically defensible? I think it was. But saying this does not provide social and educational research with any rule that will apply in all cases. What to do in specific cases is very often not going to be an easy call, and misgivings like Facio's often cannot be eliminated. To further complicate matters, in addition to differing concrete circumstances, differences in philosophical frameworks can also contribute to ethical complexity. Contra Lincoln, whatever benefits the interpretive turn has brought, an ethically simpler life for researchers is quite clearly not among them.

Reporting results

There is a further kind of increased ethical complexity engendered by the interpretive turn in social and educational research: how to report results. As before, researchers employing quantitative methods can face some of the same difficulties as those employing qualitative methods. But also as before, they are more numerous and more acute for the latter. The general source of the difficulties is the *thick* description that characterizes qualitative methods. Because such descriptions are judged for accuracy, at least in part, by how well they square with the insider's or "*emic*" perspective, researchers must negotiate or "construct" these descriptions in collaboration with research participants. (Compare negotiating statistical analyses with participants.) This raises the questions of who owns the data (e.g., Noddings, 1986) and how it may be used subsequently (e.g., Johnson, 1982), as well as the question of how much power participants should have to challenge, edit and change written reports. Except by adopting the extremes of providing participants either absolute power, or none, crafting a defensible report is a thorny ethical problem.

Thick description in reporting also complicates the protection of privacy. In contrast to survey researchers, for instance, researchers employing participant observation, interviewing, etc., can rarely, if ever, provide anonymity to research participants. Instead, they must rely on maintaining confidentiality as the means to protect privacy. The possibility sometimes exists, however remotely, that researchers could be required by a court to reveal their sources. This is a possibility to which research participants, especially "vulnerable populations" (e.g., undocumented immigrants), should be alerted.

A more pervasive threat to privacy posed by reports is that the real sites and individuals described in such reports might be identified. Various techniques to protect confidentiality, especially the use of pseudonyms, are typically employed to mask identities, but these techniques can fail (e.g., Johnson, 1982). And it is doubtful whether a more rigorous application of techniques to protect confidentiality can eliminate this problem. Population, physical geography, economic base, class stratification, and so forth, all go into to understanding a community; habits, attitudes, language, physical bearing, and so forth, of various actors all go into to understanding social life within it. These are the very kinds of things that, when reported, lead to breaches of confidentiality (see, e.g., Johnson, 1982). Unfortunately, suppressing them can only come at the cost of foregoing the value of thick description.

Breaches of confidentiality are not generally a problem unless a damaging characterization of a community or some of its members is provided. Part of the remedy is thus engaging participants in dialogue about the contents of reports in the way described previously. But this is only a partial remedy and will work only sometimes. For a damaging characterization might be called for. For instance, suppose a community (or school) and its leaders can be characterized as profoundly racist and sexist. Shouldn't such findings be reported in the interests of those who are being oppressed, at the site in question and elsewhere?

Of course, researchers must be extremely careful and deliberate about rendering such judgments, but this much is clear: The problem cannot be eliminated by casting reports in wholly *objective* (read: sterile and value-neutral) language. (This is one reading of Johnson, 1982, and a common proposal. See also Phillips and Burbules, 2000.) As description moves toward being more objective in this sense, it simultaneously moves toward *thin* description. Compare "Girls alternate between being bored and intimidated in the typical classroom discussion" with "Girls participate less than boys in the typical classroom discussion." The first description is thicker than the second, and is less objective only in the sense that it requires different (and admittedly more) evidence to substantiate. (This point is elaborated in Chapter 4.) On the other hand, it is also at least one step closer to understanding what is going on and one step closer to informing what actions might be taken to improve girls' school experience. Description and evaluation are generally related in this way in social and educational research (e.g., House & Howe, 1999; Rorty, 1982b; Scriven, 1969). The key is not to eliminate the evaluative component of descriptions, for this just dilutes them and compromises their usefulness. The key is to get the descriptions right.

Conclusion: Continuity Through Change

There is a basic discontinuity between the traditional problematic and the contemporary problematic in the ethics of social and educational research, and its sources are both epistemological-methodological and moral-political.

Under the influence of positivism, the traditional problematic is based in an epistemological-methodological framework that sees the knowledge of interest—technical, scientific, expert—as the exclusive province of research-ers. This body of knowledge, as well as research that contributes to it, are conceived to be free of moral-political content. The moral obligation of researchers to participants is focused narrowly on respecting their choice of whether or not to participate and protecting them from proximate harms.

Under the influence of interpretivism, the contemporary problematic is based in an epistemological-methodological framework that sees the knowledge of interest as the province of both researchers and participants, as collaboratively constructed by them. This body of knowledge, as well as research that contributes to it, are conceived to be thoroughly and unavoidably laden with morals and politics. The moral obligation of researchers to participants is focussed broadly on all dimensions of research.

Despite this discontinuity, is there also a basic continuity between the traditional and contemporary problematics? In particular, should the principle of autonomy be retained, or must it be jettisoned along with the rest of the framework associated with the traditional problematic? The arguments of this chapter have been aimed to show that it should be retained. Indeed, the traditional problematic does not place too much emphasis on autonomy. On the contrary, by bracketing the moral-political dimensions of research and thereby severely restricting the role of participants, the traditional problematic places too little emphasis on autonomy. However much the interpretive turn may have complicated how to understand and protect autonomy, protecting it—indeed, *fostering* it—is a fundamental concern of the contemporary problematic in the ethics of social and educational research.

The idea that basic continuities exist between traditional and contemporary perspectives on educational research, and that, accordingly, we ought to re-think rather than jettison central epistemological-political concepts—truth, objectivity, rationality, autonomy, democracy, justice—has been a recurrent theme throughout this book. The chapters addressing these issues have dovetailed and complemented one another in numerous ways. What remains to be done is to bring all of this together to underwrite a general approach to educational research. This is the project I broach in the final chapter.

Notes

1 I do not deny there may be other ways of distinguishing perspectives. For instance, feminism is perhaps conspicuous in its absence. But feminism cuts across the five perspectives. Furthermore, Noddings' care theory is one kind of feminist perspective I explicitly address.
2 This is a theme of Chapter 5. Also see, for example, Burbules and Rice's (1991) characterization of "anti-modernism."

Chapter 9

TOWARD DEMOCRATIC EDUCATIONAL RESEARCH

Educational research can never be value-free. To the extent it approaches value-freedom in its self-perception, it is to that extent dangerous. To the extent it approaches value-freedom in fact, it is to that extent useless.

This is a bold set of claims, perhaps. Thus, I begin by providing a brief justification for them before proceeding to develop the argument of this chapter. Much of this will be in the way of a review of points made in previous chapters.

The claim that educational research can never be value-*free* is not quite the same as the claim that educational research can never be value-*neutral*, at least where this is taken in a *weak* sense to mean *neutral among* different moral-political stances. For example, research on the acquisition of basic computation skills is a good candidate for the kind of investigation that can quite plausibly be characterized as neutral in this weak sense. Research on the acquisition of basic reading skills is another candidate, albeit a more controversial one. But what is important to note about examples such as these is that to the extent they may be correctly characterized as value neutral, this *neutrality doesn't go all the way down*. That is, basic computation and literacy skills are widely embraced educational values lurking below the surface. Thus, although educational research can be value neutral in the *weak* sense just discussed, it can never be value neutral in the *strong* sense of being value-free.

Why is the self-perception on the part of educational researchers of value-freedom (of value-neutrality in the strong sense) dangerous? It is dangerous because it introduces (not eliminates) the potential for bias. Concepts such as "intelligence," "achievement," "higher order thinking skills," and the like, have a general evaluative dimension (which becomes more specific when they are operationalized for the purposes of research). Such concepts are liable to bias when they are taken to pick out purely descriptive characteristics. Because they are inherently evaluative, classifying and judging persons in terms of them—as in "African Americans lag in achievement"—is evaluative as well. That is, there is no *additional* question of whether the fact that the achievement of African Americans lags is a bad thing.

Of course, one might give different explanations that locate the source bad-ness in different places. Race-based biological determinists locate it in the genes of African Americans; egalitarians locate it in unjust social arrangements. But it is the former (e.g., Murray & Herrnstein, 1994) who typically claim to be eschewing values and merely following science wherever it leads. The obser-vation that they can't really do this (i.e., they can't avoid the implicit evaluative dimensions of concepts such as intelligence and achievement) doesn't settle the matter of which explanation is the correct one. But it does preclude race-based biological determinists from claiming that they are *only* presenting the findings of science and that values are an altogether different matter. It also precludes them from evading moral responsibility for the premises and consequences of their program of research.

Because value-laden concepts cannot be avoided in educational research, the danger associated with their use cannot be eliminated. It can be significantly reduced, however, by the sort of cautious and critical attitude that characterizes the work of researchers who are conscious of how thoroughly saturated with value commitments their work is.

Why is educational research that attains value-freedom useless? Because, to attain value-freedom, it would have to employ a vocabulary that excluded value-laden concepts and that, accordingly, would have no practical import. Short of this extreme, educational research can approach value-freedom by making itself *evaluatively thin*. That is, it can avoid claims such as "Gay and Lesbian youth are oppressed" in favor of claims such as "Gay and Lesbian youth are at risk." Now, I don't want to suggest that there are never good reasons—*strategic* reasons, as I call them in the conclusion—for moderating claims in this way. The price, however, is broadening the gap between what research can tell us and what we should do *vis-à-vis* educational policy and practice. As I argued in Chapter 4, changing evaluative content merely serves to change what is being described, and changing evaluative content in the direction of value neutrality can compromise practical import. In this vein, "Gay and Lesbian youth are oppressed" better targets problems and remedies than "Gay and Lesbian youth are at risk."

The question, then, is not *whether* educational research should incorporate values; for it must. The question is *which* values it should incorporate and *how*?

I take it as a given that democratic values are prominent among those that educational research ought to incorporate, a premise not likely to be challenged in the abstract. This leaves the question of details, the question of how? In what follows I provide the rudiments of an answer.

My answer is provided in two major strands. In the first, I characterize and defend a deliberative conception of democracy (a conception of democratic decision-making, to be more precise). To be sure, this is not the only conception of democratic decision-making in which educational research might be grounded, or the most widely embraced. In this vein, I revisit some criticisms of the "emotive" conception advanced in Chapter 4. The first strand of analysis applies most naturally and straightforwardly to educational policy research. In the second strand, I suggest how the deliberative conception may also be used to, if not to direct, to at least frame educational research on curriculum, instruction, and learning.

A General Framework for Democratic Educational Research

Educational research unavoidably assumes some stance toward its role in democratic decision-making in virtue of unavoidably taking some stance toward "stakeholders:" who qualifies for participation, what their roles should be *vis-à-vis* researchers, and what their needs for and rights to information might be. There is considerable room for differences in the answers that might be given here. And matters are complicated by the fact that these questions may be asked at two levels: about the conduct of educational research itself—how democratic a practice it is—or about the relationship between educational research and other democratic bodies—how educational research serves to facilitate democratic deliberation writ large.

The idea of *democratic educational research* shouldn't be taken too literally at either of these levels. Democratic educational research can never do more than contribute to democratic deliberation writ large. Democratic decision-making is layered, and educational research is always at least one layer removed from the top. That is, it is always at least one layer removed from the outcomes of sanctioned democratic procedures such as voting or decision-making by office holders. Neither can educational research be conceived as a democratic practice unto itself. Construing democratic educational research as simply a localized democratic practice would divest it of what makes it *research* by providing no place for the expertise of researchers in formulating and guiding studies, and in analyzing and writing-up the results.

Still, there is a very significant sense in which educational research may be democratic—or fail to be. To be democratic, educational researchers should (1) assume a responsive attitude toward stakeholders and (2) seek to mitigate or eliminate obstacles to the free and equal give-and-take among stakeholders necessary for genuine democratic decision-making. And it should do this both with respect to its internal practices and with respect to the contribution it makes to the decision-making of other democratic bodies.

The dominant conception of democratic-decision making—the emotive (or preferential) conception—provides a poor framework. As discussed in

Chapter 4, this conception fails to differentiate between competing claims in terms of their moral weightiness; it holds values to be immune from rational examination; and it does not check imbalances of power. The conception of social and educational research that aligns itself with emotive democracy is "descriptive:" real "scientific" work involves no position on values. Its conclusions and recommendations connect to values only *hypothetically*: adopt policy or practice X, if value Y is to be promoted. Arguably, feeding this kind of information into the now prevailing conditions of political decision-making and then letting the chips fall where they may not only fails to mitigate or eliminate power imbalances; it exacerbates them by hiding how they drive decision-making under the cloak of "democracy."

Deliberative democratic theory provides an alternative. The fundamental elements of such a theory have existed for quite some time, in Dewey's version of liberalism, for example, and in Habermas's version of critical theory. On the current scene, it has been championed under the specific banner of deliberative democracy by thinkers such as Joshua Cohen and Amy Gutmann.

Deliberative democratic theory differs significantly from the emotive conception. Consistent with the conception of values sketched in Chapter 4, deliberative theory holds that there is something to deliberate about when it comes to values, that values are not impervious to rational investigation and dialogue. It holds that the conditions of decision-making should be designed so as to permit free and equal participation. This requires a joint commitment on the part of participants to determine what is truly right, based on argument and evidence, rather than a commitment to a *strategy* to use the power at their disposal to win assent to what they perceive is in their best interests. Rather than holding their value commitments impervious to challenge and being forced to see themselves as victims of a failed strategy when they don't win assent to their initial views, participants can actually see their value commitments change, as new, more adequate positions are "constructed" out of the material of joint deliberation.

The conception of social and educational research that aligns itself with deliberative democratic theory is "prescriptive:" real "scientific" work is shot through and through with values. Its conclusions and recommendations connect to values categorically—adopt policy or practice X—and it incorporates specific measures to eliminate or mitigate power imbalances.

Below I flesh out a conception of democratic educational research that aligns itself with deliberative democracy in terms of three principles: inclusion, dialogue, and deliberation. Before I begin, several observations are in order to help orient the discussion. First, the three principles overlap significantly, and each one could probably be conceived "thickly" enough to subsume the other two. They are distinguished for heuristic reasons. Second, the principles weave together methodological and moral-political considerations, consistent with a theme that has recurred throughout the chapters of this book. Third, the same limitations discussed above apply regarding the degree to which educational research can and ought to be literally democratic.

Inclusion

Inclusion is a principle that all educational policy research should observe. Methodologically, it is required to avoid biased samples and, thus, biased results. Democratically, it is required to ensure that all relevant voices are heard. In some cases—for example, federal support for vouchers—the relevant voices include the entire national citizenry. In other cases—for example, the reform of mathematics curricula—the assortment of relevant voices is more limited.

Inclusion, of course, comes in different degrees, ranging from the *passive* (e.g., participants filling out a fixed-response survey) to the *active* (e.g., participants engaging in face-to-face discussions). And there are many places in between, including the *representative* (e.g., educational researchers interpreting and reporting the results of their face-to-face discussions with participants). There is no general rule regarding which point along this continuum from passive to active is always best. That has to be decided on a case-by-case basis, and will depend on the existent background knowledge, the nature of the questions to be addressed, the available resources, the time-line, and so forth.

Dialogue

There is no guarantee that educational policy research will be rendered democratic solely by being inclusive. Even where research is inclusive, it can be used for the purposes of technical control rather than deliberation, particularly where inclusion is passive. Passive inclusion is not enough to ensure that the voices included will be *genuine*. This requires active inclusion, which shades into the requirement of dialogue.

Enter the interpretive turn, and the research methods that complement it. The interpretive turn emphasizes active inclusion because it emphasizes understanding people in their own terms, in their own environments. So-called "qualitative" methods are best suited for this. Participant observation, interviews, focus groups all provide means of investigating social life from the inside. Each technique involves some form of dialogue between researchers and research participants to get below surface appearances to obtain a richer and more nuanced understanding of social life.

So-called "quantitative" methods aren't altogether ruled out here, but they do have notable limitations. Take the example of fixed-response survey instruments. To get at genuine voices, such instruments must be based on the results of dialogical interactions among researchers and research participants concerning the subject matter of the instrument. Once such an instrument has been developed, however, and is then administered and analyzed, the scope of what can be learned about life from the inside is limited as a consequence of foregoing any further access to the open-endedness and unpredictability associated with the give-and-take among researchers and research participants that characterizes dialogical encounters.

But suppose the survey results are entered into new dialogical encounters, with the participants who completed the survey, some new group of participants, or both. This indicates how numerous the possibilities are and how loose the fit is between specific research methods and overarching research frameworks.

Deliberation

Whereas inclusion ranges from passive to active, dialogue ranges from *elucidating* to *critical*. And just as active inclusion shades into dialogue, critical dialogue shades into deliberation. The manner in which dialogue is structured and the information that is entered into it are all important in determining whether it is deliberative.

By "elucidating dialogue" I mean dialogue that is limited to clarifying the views and self-understandings of research participants. This way of structuring dialogue is rooted in a certain conception of the interpretive turn that gives full weight to the "insider's perspective," and that denies such a perspective can be true or false, right or wrong. It construes researchers as facilitators of dialogue rather than as active participants in it.

Guba and Lincoln exemplify this approach well (though they variously label it "naturalistic inquiry" and "constructivism"). They write:

> [The preferred method is] to negotiate meanings and interpretations with the human sources from which the data have chiefly been drawn because it is their constructions of reality that the inquirer seeks to reconstruct; because inquiry outcomes depend upon the nature and quality of the interaction between the knower and the known, epitomized in negotiations about the meaning of data; because the specific working hypotheses that might apply in a given context are best verified and confirmed by the people who inhabit that context; because respondents are in a better position to interpret the complex mutual interactions—shapings—that enter into what is observed; and because respondents can best understand and interpret the influence of local value patterns. (1985, p. 41)

Elsewhere they write:

> The object of naturalistic inquiry is to identify and describe various *emic* constructions and place those constructions in touch—with the intent of evolving a more informed and sophisticated construction than any single one of the emic constructions, or the researcher's . . . *etic* construction, represents. (1989, p. 138)

Finally, they write:

> Views are neither right nor wrong but different, depending on how the construction is formed, the context in which it is formed, and the values that undergird construction in the first place. (1989, p. 255)

This conception of dialogue promises to improve practice as a consequence of deepening mutual social understanding, but this promise cannot be realized without taking into account the structural features and causes of social practices and the norms that actors unwittingly internalize and employ in communication and action. As a consequence, this conception of dialogue is inherently conservative because, by confining itself to the insider's perspective, "it systematically ignores the possible structures of conflict within society" (Fay, 1975, p. 90) to which only researchers (outsiders) may be privy. Fay elaborates this criticism as follows:

> [This conception of dialogue] promises to reveal to the social actors what they and others are doing, thereby restoring communication by correcting the ideas that they have about each other and themselves. But this makes it sound as if all conflict (or breakdown in communication, for that matter) is generated by mistaken ideas about social reality rather than by the tensions and incompatibilities inherent in this reality itself. The upshot of this is profoundly conservative, because it leads to *reconciling people to their social order* ... (pp. 90-91)

This form of dialogue, then, puts the researcher in a relativistic predicament that provides no place for *external* criticism of the social order that had not occurred to research participants and with which they might disagree. It places the researcher in the position of being a mere data gatherer who then operates as little more than a functionary, withholding or revising her own perspective on the situation in the light of the insiders' understandings.

The conception of democratic decision-making implicit in this elucidative approach to dialogue may be suggestively described as "hyper-egalitarian" (House & Howe, 1999). Hyper-egalitarianism aspires to foster equality in dialogue among research participants, but it perverts the idea of *genuine voice* by not paying attention to the conditions out of which it can emerge. Paradoxically, it fails to mitigate, if it does not actually exacerbate, *in*equality among participants. It focuses exclusively on eliminating the possibility of bias and the abuse of power on the part of researchers by limiting their role to that of mere facilitators who must never challenge participants' views and who must eschew expert knowledge (e.g., Guba & Lincoln, 1989). It thus creates a void that may be filled by powerful—and biased—participants.

When people enter into dialogue about educational policies, they can be mistaken or misinformed about the harms and benefits of various educational policies, including to themselves. Simply clarifying how they think things work, and ought to work, can be no more than one element of genuine—or critical—dialogue. Critical dialogue includes clarifying the views and self-understandings of research participants but also subjecting these views and self-understandings to rational scrutiny. This kind of dialogue is deliberative, where deliberation is a cognitive activity in which participants and researchers collaboratively engage and from which the most rationally defensible conclusions emerge.

Of course, certain people come to deliberations with more knowledge, better sources of information, and greater facility with discursive practices than certain others do. It would be Pollyannaish in the extreme to think that people will blithely give up the strategic advantage these sources of power give them in deference to equality and determining the common good. But it would be cynical in the extreme to think that people never can nor will embrace these higher principles. The chances that they will are increased when they can be assured that these higher principles will frame deliberations and that, by adopting them, they won't thereby lose out to others who are permitted to act strategically (e.g., Rawls, 1971).

Educational researchers can give some such assurances—though no guarantees, of course—in contexts in which they have reasonable control over what participants will be included and the forums for deliberation. For example, they can monitor and direct dialogue to reduce inequality in deliberative forums. They can employ various formal devices, for example, establishing minority caucuses, to help ensure that when minority groups participate in larger forums, they do so under conditions that better approximate freedom and equality. They can insure that relevant and credible empirical evidence, both local and from the broader arena of social research, informs deliberation.

The Democratic Framework Applied to Educational Policy Research

A very small portion of educational research, including policy research, is subject to this much control by researchers and to a straightforward application of the three requirements of democratic educational research: inclusion, dialogue, and deliberation. A recent study of school choice I conducted with several colleagues (Howe & Eisenhart, 2000; Howe, Eisenhart, & Betebenner, 2001) provides one illustration of how democratic educational research works in practice. The study was commissioned by a school district in response to upheaval in the community over its school choice policy and the implications for school consolidation and closure.

Inclusion

Parents, teachers, and school administrators were identified as the primary stakeholders whose voices needed to be heard. We surveyed and conducted focus groups with a variety of school groups composed of these stakeholders across a range of levels (elementary, middle, and high) and types of district schools (choice versus neighborhood). We also conducted a random telephone survey of parents who were not active in the school district or their children's schools.

Dialogue

The primary forums for dialogue were the focus groups in individual schools. In the focus groups, we probed for participants' perspectives on how the school choice system had affected their schools, and what they believed to be the benefits and harms of school choice for the district overall. The focus groups were more like "elucidating" than "critical" dialogue, except to the extent that participants challenged one another. Only on rare occasions did the researchers challenge what participants had to say.

Deliberation

Deliberation (or "critical" dialogue) was (and continues to be) fragmented and amorphous. The study report (Howe & Eisenhart, 2000) exemplifies deliberation to the extent it challenges certain participants' views and confirms certain others' by appeal to other findings from the study (for example, statistics on racial and income stratification, and on the practice of "skimming" high performing students) and to findings from the broader arena of educational research. But the choice study has so far not resulted in any face-to-face deliberations about its findings, and whether it ever will remains to be seen. So, it is better seen as grist for deliberation than as exemplifying deliberation itself.

The value of the study's potential to stimulate deliberation should not be under estimated. There are a number of ways the choice study has contributed to deliberation about school choice policy, even if only indirectly and only within forums my colleagues and I have not designed and over which we have little control. For example, the findings were presented in a (televised) meeting with the school board and in a separate meeting with school administrators, each followed by a question and answer period that included some critical dialogue. The findings have been reported in the local newspapers, resulting in some critical dialogue among the readership. The results also have been used by a group of activists to support suggested changes in the district's funding scheme. And, reaching beyond the confines of the local community, the findings have been infused into the national conversation about school choice policies.

On the surface, there is nothing in the preceding paragraph to distinguish democratic educational research from any other that is actively disseminated and that receives some attention, including, research rooted in a *strategic* approach to democratic decision-making. The difference lies deeper, at the level of the aims educational policy research adopts and, along with this, how the problem-space is defined and what methodology is employed. How these are conceived contributes in no small way to just what the ingredients of the grist for democratic decision-making about educational policy will be.

The Democratic Framework Applied to Pedagogical Research

There is a vast array of scholarship on the relationships among democracy, education, and the subject matter and aims of pedagogical research. (For convenience, I use "pedagogical research" to refer to research on curriculum, instruction, and learning.) Due to the tendency (or prejudice) to identify the meaning of "educational research" with explicitly *empirical* educational research," I would probably mislead if I labeled this scholarship (much of which falls under labels such as "philosophy of education" and "curriculum theory") "democratic educational research." Nonetheless, the question of how empirical research on pedagogy fosters (or subverts) democracy cannot fully insulate itself from these broader philosophical questions.

Thus, a deliberative democratic framework can be applied to research on pedagogy, in addition to research on educational policy. Respecting the expertise of educators and educational researchers, however, implies a looser interpretation. In particular, the principles of inclusion, dialogue, and deliberation do not readily apply, or apply only in more attenuated forms.

John Dewey's "experimentalist" approach provides the closest approximation to a democratic approach to pedagogical research. Dewey's overarching educational goal is the creation of a truly democratic citizenry. This can best be achieved, he believed, by highly deliberative school communities who constantly engage in experimenting with subject matter and instructional techniques and who engage in ongoing dialogue about the results. The peculiarities of the social circumstances, including the make-up of students, play a major role in the research activities of such school communities. And Dewey saw an intimate connection between these kinds of communities and democracy, both intrinsically and extrinsically. That is, such communities exemplify democracy as well as instill democratic skills and virtues in their members.

Dewey's vision retains considerable merit, but it continues to be relegated to the margins. As public education is currently structured, educational researchers are rarely school insiders. They are usually outsiders, typically university faculty. And the school communities they find are much more hierarchically— and undemocratically—organized than in Dewey's conception. Under the prevailing circumstances, democratic educational researchers are usually cast in the role of outside experts, whether they choose to be or not.

As I intimated before, much of the relevant educational scholarship in this vein comes under the rubrics of "philosophy of education" and "curriculum theory"—the work of Michael Apple, Paulo Friere, Henry Giroux, bell hooks, Jane Roland Martin, Cameron McCarthy, and Nel Noddings, to give a few examples—scholarship that, for lack of a better term, employs *conceptual* rather than *empirical* evidence and argument. (This is a blurry line, indeed, both philosophically and because the findings of empirical studies may be employed in either type of analysis.) But there are numerous examples of dyed-in-the-wool empirical studies of schooling practices that take promoting or hindering democracy as central.

An illustrative collection of studies of this kind is Lois Weis and Michelle Fine's *Beyond Silenced Voices* (1993). The essays in the collection, they say, "force us to listen carefully to the *discursive underground* of students and adults that flourish within the margins of our public schools. These voices need to be heard ... if we are serious about schools as a democratic public sphere" (p. 2). How femininity, masculinity, race, and beliefs and attitudes about sexual orientation are shaped and reinforced by school cultures and curricula are among the issues with which students and teachers are engaged in dialogue by educational researchers. Among the more specific questions addressed are how certain voices are missing from the culture and curricula, what the consequences might be, and what measures might be taken in response. Although this research is not described in terms of inclusion, dialogue, and deliberation explicitly, these principles implicitly guide it.

Of course, this genre of research is heavily focused on the "hidden curriculum," which renders it highly political. Research on, say, mathematics instruction is less so. Research on mathematics instruction illustrates the limiting case of democratic educational research because it provides one of the clearest examples of the need for expert knowledge to trump democratic deliberation. That is, mathematicians, learning theorists, and mathematics educators should determine the mathematics curriculum, not inclusive democratic deliberation.

But broader questions are lurking. For example, what approaches to math curricula and instruction best prepare students to become competent democratic citizens? What approaches to math curricula and instruction are least likely to be exclusionary of certain populations? What approaches to math curricula and instruction are most likely to make students critical mathematical thinkers and to foster a healthy skepticism of mathematics as an all-purpose intellectual tool? What trade-offs are to be made among mathematics and other subjects?

Experts in mathematics, learning, and mathematics education should indeed have a major voice in formulating answers to these questions, but not the only voice. If mathematics education research is to be effective in driving practice, it will have to pay attention voices other than those of the experts—an idea gaining momentum in the mathematics education research community itself (e.g., Price, 1996; Peressini, 1998).

Final Remarks

The compatibilist-interpretivist-constructivist-transformationist-democratic methodological framework can be brought under one less cumbersome label: "pragmatic." Several pragmatic themes are central to it.

The framework evaluates methodologies not by *a priori* epistemological standards, but by the epistemological standard of their fruitfulness *in use*. In so doing, it blurs the edges among empirical research methodologies, closing the quantitative/qualitative divide. More generally, it blurs the edges between good methodology and the moral-political principles that should guide educational research, closing the fact/value divide.

The framework abandons the quest for ultimate epistemological foundations and, like most epistemological positions these days, holds that knowledge is a human construction. It also holds, however, that truth, objectivity, democracy, justice, and the like, are indispensable and redeemable ideals, without which educational research loses its rudder and falls into a self-defeating relativism. Finally, it holds that educational research should be conceived and conducted so as to live up to what a *genuine* form of democracy requires.

References

Griswold v. Connecticut, 381 U.S. 479 (1964).

Roe v. Wade, 410 U.S. 113 (1973).

Aronowitz, S., & Giroux, H. (1991). *Postmodern education.* Minneapolis, MN: University of Minnesota Press.

Barber, B. (1992). *An aristocracy of everyone.* New York: Ballantine Books.

Beauchamp, T. L., Faden, R. R., Wallace, R. J., & Walters, L. (1982). Introduction. In T. L. Beauchamp, R. R. Faden, R. J. Wallace, & L. Walters (Eds.), *Ethical issues in social science research* (pp. 3–39). Baltimore, MD: The Johns Hopkins University Press.

Benhabib, S. (1995). Feminism and postmodernism. In L. Nicholson (Ed.), *Feminist contentions* (pp. 17–34). New York: Routledge.

Bernstein, R. (1983). *Beyond objectivism and relativism.* Philadelphia: University of Pennsylvania Press.

Bernstein, R. (1996, April). *Pragmatism and postmodernism: The relevance of John Dewey.* Paper presented at the annual meeting of the American Educational Research Association, New York.

Burbules, N. (1993). *Dialogue in teaching.* New York: Teachers College Press.

Burbules, N., & Rice, S. (1991). Dialogue across difference: Continuing the conversation. *Harvard Educational Review, 61*(4), 393–416.

Campbell, D. (1974, September). *Qualitative knowing in action research.* Kurt Lewin Award Address, Society for the Psychological Study of Social Issues. Presented at the annual meeting of the American Psychological Association, New Orleans.

Campbell, D. (1979). Degrees of freedom and the case study. In T. Cook & C. Reichardt (Eds.), *Qualitative and quantitative methods in evaluation research* (pp. 49–67). Beverly Hills, CA: Sage.

Campbell, D. (1982). Experiments as arguments. In E. R. House, S. Mathison, J. A. Pearsol, & H. Preskill (Eds.), *Evaluation studies review annual* (Vol. 7, pp. 117–128). Beverly Hills, CA: Sage.

Caplan, A. (1982). On privacy and confidentiality in social science research. In T. L. Beauchamp, R. R. Faden, R. J. Wallace, & L. Walters (Eds.), *Ethical issues in social science research* (pp. 315–328). Baltimore, MD: The Johns Hopkins University Press.

Code, L. (1993). Taking subjectivity into account. In L. Alcoff & E. Potter (Eds.), *Feminist epistemologies* (pp. 15–48). New York: Routledge.

Coleman, J. (1968). The concept of equal educational opportunity. *Harvard Educational Review, 38*(1), 7–22.

Collins, P. H. (1991). Learning from the outsider within: The sociological significance of black feminist thought. In M. Fonow & J. Cook (Eds.), *Beyond methodology: Feminist scholarship and lived research* (pp. 35–59). Bloomington, IN: Indiana University Press.

Connell, R. W. (1987). *Gender and power.* Stanford, CA: Stanford University Press.

Cornett, J., & Chase, S. (1989, March). *The analysis of teacher thinking and the problem of ethics: Reflections of a case study participant and a naturalistic researcher.* Paper presented at the annual meeting of the American Educational Research Association, San Francisco.

Daniels, N. (1979). Wide reflective equilibrium and theory acceptance in ethics. *Journal of Philosophy, 6*(5), 256–282.

Davidson, D. (1973). On the very idea of a conceptual scheme. *Proceedings of the American Philosophical Association, 68,* 5–20.

Dennis, R. (1993). Participant observations. In J. Stanfield & R. Dennis (Eds.), *Race and ethnicity in research methods* (pp. 53–74). Newbury Park, CA: Sage.

Denzin, N. (1989). *The research act: A theoretical introduction to sociological methods* (3rd ed.). Englewood Cliffs, NJ: Prentice-Hall.

Dewey, J. (1938). *Experience and education.* New York: Macmillan Publishing Company.

Elgin, C. (1997). *Between the absolute and the arbitrary.* Ithaca, NY: Cornell University Press.

Ellsworth, E. (1992). Why doesn't this feel empowering. In C. Luke & J. Gore (Eds.), *Feminisms and critical pedagogy* (pp. 90–119). New York: Routledge.

Erickson, F. (1982). Taught cognitive learning in its immediate environments: A neglected topic in the anthropology of education. *Anthropology and Education Quarterly, 13*(2), 149–180.

Facio, E. (1993). Ethnography as personal experience. In J. Stanfield & R. Dennis (Eds.), *Race and ethnicity in research methods* (pp. 74–91). Newbury Park, CA: Sage.

Fay, B. (1975). *Social theory and political practice.* Birkenhead, Great Britian: George Allen and Unwin, Ltd.

Fay, B. (1987). *Critical social science.* Ithaca, NY: Cornell University Press.

Foucault, M. (1970). *Discipline and punish: The birth of the prison.* New York: Vintage Books.

Foucault, M. (1987). Questions of method: An interview with Michel Foucault. In K. Baynes, J. Bohman, & T. McCarthy (Eds.), *After philosophy: End or transformation?* (pp. 100–117). Cambridge, MA: MIT Press.

Frazer, N. (1995). Pragmatism, feminism and the linguistic turn. In L. Nicholson (Ed.), *Feminist contentions* (pp. 157–171). New York: Routledge.

Garrison, J. (1986). Some principles of postpositivistic philosophy of science. *Educational Researcher, 15*(9), 12–18.

Garrison, J. (1994). Realism, deweyan pragmatism, and educational research. *Education Researcher, 23*(1), 5–14.

Gates, H. L. (1992). *Loose canons.* New York: Oxford University Press.

Geertz, C. (1979). From the native's point of view: On the nature of anthropological understanding. In P. Rabinow & W. Sullivan (Eds.), *Interpretive social science* (pp. 225–242). Berkeley: University of California Press.

Giddens, A. (1976). *New rules of sociological method.* New York: Basic Books.

Glasersfeld, E. von. (1995). *Radical constructivism: A way of knowing and learning.* London: The Falmer Press.

Glasersfeld, E. von. (1996). Introduction: Aspects of constructivism. In C. Fosnot (Ed.), *Constructivism: Theory, perspectives, and practice.* New York: Teachers College Press.

Goldman, A. (1995). Naturalistic epistemology. In R. Audi (Ed.), *The Cambridge dictionary of philosophy* (pp. 518–519). New York: Cambridge University Press.

Goodnow, J. (1984). On being judged intelligent. *International Journal of Psychology, 19,* 391–406.

Gould, S. J. (1981). *The mismeasure of man.* New York: W. W. Norton & Company.

Gruender, D. (1996). Constructivism and learning: A philosophical appraisal. *Educational Technology, 36*(3), 21–29.

Guba, E. (1987). What have we learned about naturalistic evaluation? *Evaluation Practice, 8*(1), 23–43.

Guba, E., & Lincoln, Y. (1985). *Naturalistic inquiry.* Beverly Hills, CA: Sage.

Guba, E., & Lincoln, Y. (1989). *Fourth generation evaluation.* Newbury Park, CA: Sage.

Gutmann, A. (1994). Introduction. In A. Gutmann (Ed.), *Multiculturalism: Examining the politics of recognition* (pp. 3–24). Princeton, NJ: Princeton University Press.

Hacking, I. (1999). *The social construction of what?* Cambridge, MA: Harvard University Press.

Harding, S. (1993). Rethinking standpoint epistemology: What is "strong objectivity"? In L. Alcoff & E. Potter (Eds.), *Feminist epistemologies* (pp. 49–80). New York: Routledge.

Haworth, K. (1997, May 30). Clinton starts efforts to recruit minority volunteers for federal research projects. *The Chronicle of Higher Education,* p. A39.

Heshusius, L. (1994). Freeing ourselves from objectivity: Managing subjectivity by turning toward a participatory mode or consciousness? *Educational Researcher, 23*(3), 15–22.

House, E. (1980). *Evaluating with validity.* Beverly Hills, CA: Sage.

House, E., & Howe, K. (1999). *Values in evaluation and social research.* Thousand Oaks, CA: Sage.

Howe, K. (1985). Two dogmas of educational research. *Educational Researcher, 14*(8), 10–18.

Howe, K. (1988). Against the quantitative-qualitative incompatibility thesis (or dogmas die hard). *Educational Researcher, 17*(8), 10–16.

Howe, K. (1992). Getting over the quantitative-qualitative debate. *American Journal of Education, 100*(2), 236–256.

Howe, K. (1997). *Understanding equal educational opportunity: Social justice, democracy, and schooling.* New York: Teachers College Press.

Howe, K. (1998). What (epistemic) benefit inclusion? In S. Laird (Ed.), *Philosophy of education 1997* (pp. 89–96). Normal, IL: Philosophy of Education Society.

Howe, K., & Dougherty, K. (1993). Ethics, IRB's, and the changing face of educational research. *Educational Researcher, 22*(9), 16–21.

Howe, K., & Eisenhart, M. (1990). Standards for qualitative (and quantitative) research: A prologomenon. *Educational Researcher, 19*(4), 2–9.

Howe, K., & Eisenhart, M. (2000). *A study of Boulder Valley School District's open enrollment system* (Tech. Rep.). Boulder, CO: Author.

Howe, K., Eisenhart, M., & Betebenner, D. (2001). School choice crucible: A case study of Boulder Valley. *Phi Delta Kappan, 83*(2), 137–146.

Howe, K., & Moses, M. (1999). Ethics in educational research. In A. Iran-Nejad & P. D. Pearson (Eds.), *Review of research of education* (Vol. 24, pp. 21–60). Washington, D. C.: American Educational Research Association.

Huberman, M. (1987). How well does educational research really travel? *Educational Researcher, 16*(1), 5–13.

Jackson, P. (1968). *Life in classrooms.* New York: Holt, Rinehart, and Winston.

James, W. (1968). Pragmatism's conception of the truth. In *Essays in pragmatism* (pp. 100–150). New York: Hafner Publishing Company.

Jayaratne, T., & Stewart, A. (1991). Quantitative and qualitative methods in the social sciences: Current feminist issues and practical strategies. In M. Fonow & J. Cook (Eds.), *Beyond methodology: Feminist scholarship and lived research* (pp. 107–118). Bloomington, IN: Indiana University Press.

Johnson, C. (1982). Risks in the publication of fieldwork. In J. Sieber (Ed.), *The ethics of social research: Fieldwork, regulation, and publication* (pp. 71–92). New York: Springer-Verlag.

Kaplan, A. (1964). *The conduct of inquiry.* San Francisco: Chandler.

Kelman, H. (1982). Ethical issues in different social science methods. In T. L. Beauchamp, R. R. Faden, R. J. Wallace, & L. Walters (Eds.), *Ethical issues in social science research* (pp. 40–100). Baltimore: The Johns Hopkins University Press.

Kozol, J. (1991). *Savage inequalities.* New York: Crown.

Kuhn, T. (1962). *The structure of scientific revolutions.* Chicago: University of Chicago Press.

Kuhn, T. (1977). *The essential tension: Selected studies in scientific tradition and change.* Chicago: University of Chicago Press.

Kymlicka, W. (1990). *Contemporary political theory: An introduction.* New York: Oxford University Press.

Kymlicka, W. (1991). *Liberalism, community and culture.* New York: Oxford University Press.

Lather, P. (1991a). *Getting smart: Feminist research and pedagogy with/in postmodernism.* New York: Routledge.

Lather, P. (1991b). Post-critical pedagogies: A feminist reading. *Education and Society, 9*(2), 100–111.

Lather, P. (1994). Fertile obsession: Validity after poststructuralism. In A. Gitlin (Ed.), *Power and method: Political activism in educational research* (pp. 36–60). New York: Routledge.

Laudan, L. (1996). *Beyond postivism and relativism.* Boulder, CO: Westview Press.

Lincoln, Y. (1990). Toward a categorical imperative for qualitative research. In E. Eisner & A. Peshkin (Eds.), *Qualitative inquiry in educational research: The continuing debate* (pp. 277–295). New York: Teachers College Press.

Lindblom, C. E. (1977). *Politics and markets.* New York: Basic Books.

Longino, H. (1993). Subjects, power and knowledge: Description and prescription in feminist philosophies of science. In L. Alcoff & E. Potter (Eds.), *Feminist epistemologies* (pp. 101–120). New York: Routledge.

Lyon, D. (1994). *Postmodernity.* Minneapolis: University of Minnesota Press.

Lyotard, J. (1987). The postmodern condition. In K. Baynes, J. Bohman, & T. McCarthy (Eds.), *After philosophy: End or transformation?* (pp. 67–94). Cambridge, MA: MIT Press.

MacIntyre, A. (1981). *After virtue.* Notre Dame, IN: University of Notre Dame Press.

MacIntyre, A. (1982). Risk, harm, and benefit assessments as instruments of moral evaluation. In T. L. Beauchamp, R. R. Faden, R. J. Wallace, & L. Walters (Eds.), *Ethical issues in social science research* (pp. 175–192). Baltimore: The Johns Hopkins University Press.

MacKenzie, B. (1977). *Behaviorism and the limits of scientific method.* Atlantic Highlands, NJ: Humanities Press.

MacKinnon, C. (1989). *Toward a feminist theory of the state.* Cambridge, MA: Harvard University Press.

Madaus, G. (1994). A technological and historical consideration of equity issues associated with proposals to change the nation's testing policy. *Harvard Educational Review, 64*(1), 76–95.

Matthews, M. (1993). A problem with constructivist epistemology. In H. A. Alexander (Ed.), *Philosophy of education 1992* (pp. 303–311). Urbana, IL: Philosophy of Education Society.

McCarthy, C. (1993). Beyond the poverty in race relations: Nonsynchrony and social difference in education. In L. Weis & M. Fine (Eds.), *Beyond silenced voices* (pp. 325–346). New York: State University of New York Press.

Melden, A. I. (1966). Free actions. In B. Berofsky (Ed.), *Free will and determinism* (pp. 198–220). New York: Harper and Row.

Messick, S. (1989). Validity. In R. L. Linn (Ed.), *Educational measurement* (3rd ed., pp. 13–103). New York: American Council on Education and Macmillan.

Milgram, S. (1974). *Obedience to authority.* New York: Harper & Row.

Moser, P. (1995). Epistemology. In R. Audi (Ed.), *The Cambridge dictionary of philosophy* (pp. 233–238). New York: Cambridge University Press.

Murphy, M., & Johannsen, A. (1990). Ethical obligations and federal regulations in ethnographic research and anthropological education. *Human Organization, 49*(2), 127–134.

Murray, C., & Herrnstein, R. (1994). *The bell curve.* New York: The Free Press.

Nagel, T. (1986). *The view from nowhere.* New York: Oxford University Press.

Noddings, N. (1984). *Caring: A feminine approach to ethics and moral education.* Berkeley: University of California Press.

Noddings, N. (1986). Fidelity in teaching, teacher education, and research on teaching. *Harvard Educational Review, 56*(4), 496–510.

Nozick, R. (1974). *Anarchy, state, and utopia.* New York: Basic Books.

Ornstein, P. (1995). *Schoolgirls.* New York: Anchor Books.

Passmore, J. (1967). Logical positivism. In P. Edwards (Ed.), *The encyclopedia of philosophy* (Vol. 5, pp. 52–57). New York: The Free Press.

Peressini, D. (1998). The portrayal of parents in the reform of mathematics education: Locating the context for parental involvement. *Journal for Research in Mathematics Education, 29*(5), 555–582.

Peshkin, A. (1988). In search of subjectivity—one's own. *Educational Researcher, 17*(7), 17–21.

Phillips, D. C. (1987). *Philosophy, science, and social inquiry.* New York: Pergamon.

Phillips, D. C. (1995). The good, the bad, and the ugly: The many faces of constructivism. *Educational Researcher, 24*(7), 5–12.

Phillips, D. C., & Burbules, N. (2000). *Postpositivism and educational research.* New York: Rowman & Littlefield.

Price, J. (1996). President's report: Building bridges of mathematical understanding for all children. *Journal for Research in Mathematics Education, 27,* 603–608.

Punch, M. (1986). *The politics and ethics of fieldwork.* Beverly Hills, CA: Sage.

Putnam, H. (1990). *Realism with a human face.* Cambridge, MA: Harvard University Press.

Quine, W. V.. (1962). *From a logical point of view* (2nd ed.). Cambridge, MA: Harvard University Press.

Quine, W. V.. (1969). Epistemology naturalized. In *Ontological relativity and other essays* (pp. 69–90). New York: Columbia University Press.

Quine, W. V. O. (1970). The basis of conceptual schemes. In C. Landesman (Ed.), *The foundations of knowledge* (pp. 160–172). Englewood Cliffs, NJ: Prentice Hall.

Rabinow, P., & Sullivan, W. (1979). The interpretive turn: Emergence of an approach. In P. Rabinow & W. Sullivan (Eds.), *Interpretive social science* (pp. 1–21). Los Angeles: University of California Press.

Rawls, J. (1971). *A theory of justice.* Cambridge, MA: The Belmont Press.

Reichardt, C., & Cook, T. (1979). Beyond qualitative versus quantitative methods. In T. Cook & C. Reichardt (Eds.), *Qualitative and quantitative methods in evaluation research* (pp. 7–32). Beverly Hills, CA: Sage.

Roman, L. (1993). Double exposure: The politics of feminist materialist ethnography. *Educational Theory, 43*(3), 279–308.

Rorty, R. (1979). *Philosophy and the mirror of nature.* Princeton, NJ: Princeton University Press.

Rorty, R. (1982a). Introduction: Pragmatism and philosophy. In *Consequences of pragmatism* (p. xiii-xvii). Minneapolis: University of Minnesota Press.

Rorty, R. (1982b). Method, social science, and social hope. In *Consequences of pragmatism* (pp. 191–210). Minneapolis: University of Minnesota Press.

Rorty, R. (1982c). Pragmatism, relativism and irrationalism. In *Consequences of pragmatism* (pp. 160–175). Minneapolis: University of Minnesota Press.

Rushton, P. (1982). Moral cognition, behaviorism and social learning theory. *Ethics, 92*, 459–467.

Scheurich, J., & Young, M. (1997). Coloring epistemologies: Are our research epistemologies racially biased? *Educational Researcher, 26*(4), 4–16.

Scriven, M. (1969). Logical positivism and the behavioral sciences. In P. Achinstein & S. Barker (Eds.), *The legacy of logical positivism* (pp. 195–210). Baltimore: Johns Hopkins University Press.

Scriven, M. (1972). Objectivity and subjectivity in educational research. In L. Thomas & H. Richey (Eds.), *Philosophical redirection of educational research, the seventy-first yearbook of the National Society for the Study of Education* (pp. 94–142). Chicago: University of Chicago Press.

Scriven, M. (1983). *The evaluation taboo.* San Francisco: Jossey-Bass.

Searle, J. (1995). *The construction of social reality.* New York: The Free Press.

Shadish, W., Cook, T., & Leviton, L. (1995). *Foundations of program evaluation.* Thousand Oaks, CA: Sage.

Shepard, L. (1993). Evaluating test validity. In L. Darling Hammond (Ed.), *Review of research in education* (Vol. 19, pp. 405–450). Washington, D. C.: American Educational Research Association.

Shulman, L. (1988). Disciplines of inquiry in education: An overview. In R. Jaeger (Ed.), *Complementary methods for research in education* (pp. 3–17). Washington, D. C.: American Educational Research Association.

Siegel, H. (1996). What price inclusion? In A. Neiman (Ed.), *Philosophy of education 1995* (pp. 1–22). Normal, IL: Philosophy of Education Society.

Smith, J. K. (1983a). Quantitative versus interpretive: The problem of conducting social inquiry. In E. House (Ed.), *Philosophy of evaluation* (pp. 27–52). San Francisco: Jossey-Bass.

Smith, J. K. (1983b). Quantitative versus qualitative research: An attempt to clarify the issue. *Educational Researcher, 12*(3), 6–13.

Smith, J. K., & Heshusius, L. (1986). Closing down the conversation: The end of the quantitative-qualitative debate among educational researchers. *Educational Researcher, 15*(1), 4–12.

Smith, L. M. (1990). Ethics of qualitative field research: An individual perspective. In E. W. Eisner & A. Peshkin (Eds.), *Qualitative inquiry in education: The continuing debate* (pp. 258–276). New York: Teachers College Press.

Stanfield, J. (1993). Epistemological considerations. In J. Stanfield & R. Denis (Eds.), *Race and ethnicity in research methods* (pp. 16–38). Newbury Park, CA: Sage.

Taylor, C. (1964). *The explanation of behaviour.* New York: The Humanities Press.

Taylor, C. (1987). Interpretation and the sciences of man. In P. Rabinow & W. Sullivan (Eds.), *Interpretive social science: A second look* (pp. 33–81). Los Angeles: University of California Press.

Taylor, C. (1994). The politics of recognition. In A. Gutmann (Ed.), *Multiculturalism: Examining the politics of recognition* (pp. 25–74). Princeton, NJ: Princeton University Press.

Taylor, C. (1995a). Explanation and practical reason. In *Philosophical arguments* (pp. 34–60). Cambridge, MA: Harvard University Press.

Taylor, C. (1995b). Overcoming epistemology. In *Philosophical arguments* (pp. 1–19). Cambridge, MA: Harvard University Press.

Toulmin, S. (1953). *The philosophy of science.* New York: Harper & Row.

Usher, R., & Edwards, R. (1994). *Postmodernism and education.* New York: Routledge.

Walzer, M. (1983). *Spheres of justice.* New York: Basic books.

Wax, M. (1982). Research reciprocity rather than informed consent in fieldwork. In J. Sieber (Ed.), *The ethics of social research: Fieldwork, regulation, and publication* (pp. 33–48). New York: Springer-Verlag.

Weis, L., & Fine, M. (1993). Introduction. In L. Weis & M. Fine (Eds.), *Beyond silenced voices: Class, race, and gender in united states schools* (pp. 1–8). Albany, NY: State University of New York Press.

Werner, R. (1983). Ethical realism. *Ethics, 93,* 653–679.

Wilson, J. (1967). What is moral education? In J. Wilson, N. Williams, & B. Sugarman (Eds.), *Introduction to moral education.* Baltimore: Penguin Books.

Wilson, J. (1983). A letter from oxford. *Harvard Educational Review, 53,* 190–94.

Wittgenstein, L. (1958). *Philosophical investigations* (3rd ed.). New York: Macmillan.

Young, I. M. (1990a). Humanism, gynocentrism, and feminist politics. In *Throwing like a girl and other essays in philosophy and social theory* (pp. 73–91). Bloomington, IN: Indiana University Press.

Young, I. M. (1990b). Polity and group difference: A critique of the ideal of universal citizenship. In C. Sunstein (Ed.), *Feminism and political theory* (pp. 117–142). Chicago: The University of Chicago Press.

Young, R. (1990). *A critical theory of education.* New York: Teachers College Press.

Index

"shift", 17, 88
as absent from social science, 27n
cliques, 44
epistemological, *see* Epistemology, paradigm
Passmore, J., 26
Peressini, D., 143
Peshkin, A., 106, 107
Phillips, D.C., 38, 42, 82, 94n, 129
Politics of difference, *see also* Liberal theory, and the politics of difference; Marxism, and the politics of difference
postmodernism vs. transformationism, 77–79
Positivism, 35
analytic/synthetic distinction, 26n
and pre-interpreted categories in social research, 8, 102
and technical control, 78, 121
and the means-ends bifurcation, 121–122
as undemocratic, 122
and the fact/value dogma, *see* Fact/value dogma, roots in positivism
and the quantitative/qualitative dogma, *see* Quantitative/qualitative dogma, roots in positivism
and value-freedom, *see* Fact/value dogma, roots in positivism
as a biased epistemology, *see* Bias, epistemological
as dominant in educational research, 1
as moribund, 3, 16
as spawning the two dogmas, 2
logical, 15, 26n
scientific inference, 15, 20–21
and confirmation, 20
as the same in natural and social science, 15, 20, 21
theory vs. observation, 2, 18
verificationism, 2, 26n
Post-positivism, 18, 20–22, 26n, 44
scientific inference, 20–21
Postmodernism, 9, *see also* Compatibilism, between postmodernists and transformationists; Constructivism, and postmodernism; Deconstruction, postmodernist; Epistemology, moral; Interpretivism, the interpretive turn; Ontology of the self, postmodernist conception; Research ethics, postmodernism; Subjectivity, emphasis on shared by postmodernists and transformationists
"critical vs. "apolitical", 77
"strong" vs. "weak", 67

and relativism, 5, 67, 68
and the politics of difference, 77
as *anti*-epistemology, 101
as discontinuous with the Enlightenment, 68
as self-defeating, 6, 68, 131n
defined, 66
incredulity toward "meta- narratives", 67
Power, political
and social researchers, 10, 23, 41, 121, 139
imbalances of, 4
and research ethics, 126
as mitigated by social research, 6, 11, 78, 108, 121, 136, *see also* Democracy in educational research, deliberative
as served by social research, 4, 52, 54, 55, 62, 127, 136, 139, *see also* Democracy in educational research, emotive, hyper-egalitarian
vs. knowledge, 5, 8, 68, 78, *see also* Truth, "regimes" of
Pragmatism, *see also* Compatibilism; Epistemology, anti-foundationalism
and democracy, 144
and relativism, 7, 43
and truth, *see* Truth, pragmatic conception
as blurring methodological-epistemological edges, 11, 143
as blurring methodological-epistemological vs. moral-political edges, 11, 144
criteria of theory choice, 43, 88
Price, J., 143
Privacy, *see* Research ethics
Punch, M., 128
Putnam, H., 7, 39, 43, 86, 87, 90

Qualitative research methods, *see also* Compatibilism, and data; Description, *thick*; Dialogue, and qualitative methods; Quantitative/qualitative dogma; Research ethics, the contemporary problematic
and the insider's perspective, 31, 44, 108, 124
as congenial to feminists, 106
as ethically hazardous, 125, 127
as interpretivist, 2, 16, 30
as intimate, 9, 124
as open-ended, 9, 33, 124, 125
as subjective, 15–17
Quantitative research methods, *see also* Compatibilism, and data; Dialogue, and quantitative methods; Quantitative/qualitative dogma; Research ethics, the traditional problematic

DATE DUE

GAYLORD PRINTED IN U.S.A.